Mireille Gansel

SOUL HOUSE

Translated from French
by Joan Seliger Sidney

Preface by Fanny Howe
Afterword by Michèle Ganem Gumpel

 WORLD POETRY

Soul House
Copyright © Mireille Gansel, 2018, 2023
English translation copyright © Joan Seliger Sidney, 2023
Preface copyright © Fanny Howe, 2023
Afterword © Michèle Ganem Gumpel, 2023

Originally published as *Maison d'Âme* by
Éditions de la Coopérative (Paris, 2018).

First Edition, First Printing, 2023
ISBN 978-1-954218-17-8

World Poetry Books
New York, NY
www.worldpoetrybooks.com

Distributed in the US by SPD/Small Press Distribution
www.spdbooks.org

Distributed in the UK and Europe by Turnaround Publisher Services
www.turnaround-uk.com

Library of Congress Control Number: 2023940432

Cover Art: *untitled painting* by Lebadang (1921, Vietnam–2015, France). Etching in relief, watercolor on paper. Photographer: Luc Ho. Courtesy of Myshu Labadang's Collection. All rights reserved.

Cover design by Andrew Bourne
Typesetting by Don't Look Now
Printed in Lithuania by BALTO Print

World Poetry Books is committed to publishing exceptional translations of poetry from a broad range of languages and traditions, bringing the work of modern masters, emerging voices, and pioneering innovators from around the world to English-language readers in affordable trade editions. Founded in 2017, World Poetry Books is a 501(c)(3) nonprofit and charitable organization based in New York City and affiliated with the Humanities Institute and the Translation Program at the University of Connecticut (Storrs).

Table of Contents

Preface by Fanny Howe	ix
to inhabit beauty	21
the oustau	23
post-script	25
of these beauties that make the world habitable	27
an interior house	29
nomadic house	31
a house over there	39
leave no trace	41
to the parting of the waters	43
mu'allaqāt: the hanging odes	45
house of words	47
words as shelter	49
like so many little houses where one learns to inhabit the world	51
rainbow house	53
small fairground stalls	55
a shelter to deposit a soul's word	61
like a house of wind	63
to make a word habitable	65
post-script	73
no-place	75
a voice… like a house	77
to inhabit the words	79
small houses in the night	81

house of earth house of silk	83
these rose gardens in the days of silk weavers	89
to inhabit beauty against all odds	91
the doors of the nomads' caravans torn off	97
house of tears and light	99
stones of light	101
the bare walls of the house	103
an open door	107
the kitchen wall	109
on a snowy night	111
the light of words	115
le Paradou	117
speech of the soul	121
[it was in these lands such cold lands...]	123
a house for all horizons	125
a house to come back to against all odds	127
Skokholm Island mid-June	129
puffins	131
storm petrel	133
English puffins	135
like a message to N.D. ...	137
Farne Islands early August	139
Damask Rose petals and perfume	141
night	143
the meeting point	145
post-script: notes on a trip to Basel ...	147

Afterword by Michèle Ganem Gumpel 151

Notes to the poems 159

Acknowledgments 161

Preface

MIREILLE GANSEL WAS BORN in 1947 in the Savoie region of France where her parents had arrived as refugees at the end of World War II. In her imagination, the river Danube flashed between trees and buildings on its way to the sea and back. Other nearby cities filled up with displaced people from all around Europe where their homes had been shelled to dust. Multiple languages filled the schools and stores. Mireille's father was a Hungarian Jew. Her parents spoke German, but their neighbors spoke other languages from occupied countries.

This way Gansel began a life of listening to varieties of speech in her youth. She traveled to East Berlin in the 1960s, sat in on Brecht's rehearsals with The Berliner Ensemble doing Hölderlin's *Antigone*. Then, in the 1970s, she went to Vietnam to learn the language and live with the victims of an ongoing, vicious, unjust war. Her sources were Vietnamese people, poets. What she learned from immersion in their town, their domestic lives, language and families was the intimate correspondence between poetry and common speech.

This was her special method: to meet the poet wherever possible on their own turf, in their own town and house before translating their poems. She translated poems by Tô Hữu and found her vocation.

Much travel followed, political action, an immersion in the world she inhabited through the languages studied up close and open to readers. This life is the source of her poetic thinking and, too, her understanding of populations driven away from home by social catastrophe. In the wake of clamor and sorrow, she read Brecht, Rilke, Hölderlin, Rene Char, Nelly Sachs and translated them for unknown "others." She rarely

used this deadly term (other) and instead her mission was to reflect upon the many people who have become immigrant, who are the dis-othered world of the twenty-first century.

One moment of insight came when she realized that she—herself, the nomadic reader—was as much an alien as her subject. This moment speaks as if it were mass consciousness awakening, a rock turning over, a voice emerging from the night. It was an insight that has beamed in on philosophy, perhaps occasioned by the arrival of women like Edith Stein, Hannah Arendt, and Julia Kristeva. The word "stranger" was soon accompanied by an uncanny and a horrifying awareness of the human condition as unknowable. Translation was an action against alienation.

Gansel begins this book with her own experience of childhood. As she later wrote of poet Nelly Sachs: "The child is the common thread running through all her books." The child and first words, the child and its acute awareness of sound and sense, and of how things came to be named. Gansel called language "the underground springs of a people's hinterland." And she went forth into the world to decipher and interpret the words she heard so that she could understand them. She carried poetry out of the ruins, the way Persephone brought flowers to hell with her.

I suppose poetry enables little languages whispered in kitchens and fields to flourish. It doesn't care about order and uniformity, only about the ways of the mind. You do feel it whispering its way up the busy words of a brain otherwise occupied. The hiss of lips compressed on a word. Surrealism is a natural outcome, especially when the absurdity of war reverberates in the household. Gansel is the inheritor of a generation of such war-time and war-born thinkers as Walter Benjamin, Beckett, Hannah Arendt, Simone Weil, Edith Stein, Ludwig Wittgenstein. To follow her journal is to be led

to see where we stand today—in a future that was already germinating in thought. The recapitulation of a life experience will necessarily be jagged and punctured. The style Gansel has adopted for her translations sometimes has this fractured quality and her translator, Joan Seliger Sidney, allows some defamiliarization to enter a sentence so that the unperfected present of the new version wobbles. So some return to iambic. ("A word where beats the heart of hospitality.") Sidney allows an old-fashioned phrase into the otherwise contemporary line as if to remind the reader that the past is not over yet.

Gansel has let us accompany her from childhood to late life during a historical time which included the death of God and animals, epic bombardments of cities and oceans, and uprootedness that continues to this day. With the unsentimental intelligence of an Arendt, she brings us to the brink of a new intuition about our troubles. We are creators of our own disappearance. This double thrust is already scraped into stone and pottery

Translation has been called "resurrection" in some Hindu cultures. It does, in fact, feel as impossible as that. You carry each word out of its original form and context. Will you ever know if the word you brought can be absorbed into a new common line. Wittgenstein believed the soul lived outside of the body. Such a soul could house a body. And the person wearing the soul could decorate it with radiant senses from the living world. Colors and fragrance, music and touch. Each experience in this book flashes its tiny insight like a peacock feather. And this way it waves the evil off. Here we remember the Greek gods and are glad they may be returning.

It is in that spirit that we come to *Soul House*. Watch it unfold, as poems do, unnoticed and therefore free. Delight in objects, attention to the meanings of growth and destruction,

a commitment to the childhood of the children. Only the imprisoned know what freedom really means. A spoken word, translated into a written word, and vice versa, reminds me of the wandering poem from Arabia that Gansel includes in her book: *Full of doubts, I stopped in pastures, seeking the trace of his camels... do you remember, my sad soul, where was his tent?*

Fanny Howe
May 2023

Maison d'âme

Soul House

pour Hannah Gaspard Martin

For Hannah Gaspard Martin

> *« envers et contre tout, la maison nous invite à dire : je serai un habitant du monde malgré le monde »*
> **Gaston Bachelard**

against all odds, the house invites us to say: I will be a citizen of the world despite the world
      Gaston Bachelard

habiter la beauté

« elle était jolie ta maison, quand tu étais petite ? »
oui ta question d'enfant ce matin de printemps et soudain la beauté est une maison où habiter peut-être la première peut-être la seule –

envers et contre tout –

to inhabit beauty

"was it pretty your house, when you were little?"
yes your child's question this spring morning and suddenly
beauty is a house one inhabits perhaps the first one perhaps
the only one—

against all odds—

l'oustau

ce même printemps ta question m'a accompagnée en Pays d'Arles parmi les senteurs des jasmins et l'éclat bleuté des acanthes où j'ai retrouvé avec bonheur le nom provençal de la maison l'oustau –

un mot où bat le cœur de l'hospitalité –

the oustau

this same spring your question accompanied me to the countryside of Arles among the scent of jasmine and the bluish glow of the acanthus where happily I found again the Provençal name for the house, *l'oustau—*

a word in which the heart of hospitality beats—

post-scriptum

I

ce matin tandis que j'allais chercher des fleurs de fin d'été
chez le fleuriste sur les quais soudain le regard de ce jeune
garçon avec sa mère elle a un fichu noué comme les femmes
tziganes qui nous avaient offert l'hospitalité lui et elle en hâte
tous deux tâtent les sacs noirs dans une grande poubelle il
traîne une vieille valise entr'ouverte en tissus à carreaux –

la dignité de ce regard –

II

c'était en revenant du marché aux fleurs soudain au coin du
quai et de la passerelle de l'île Saint-Louis sous les hautes
fenêtres où passe l'ombre de Jankélévitch et d'Edmond Fleg
cette mélodie des Balkans sur son accordéon le temps juste le
temps en passant d'échanger des paroles sur ici et son pays
et quand il fait trop froid ce café brûlant qu'il prend à deux
mains il dit, il partage une cave, et aussi, non, pas un endroit
pour des fleurs, et il rit presque, et reprend la mélodie des
Balkans –

post-script

I

this morning while I was headed to the docks looking for the last phlox of summer at the florist suddenly the look of this young boy with his mother her head scarf knotted like the Romani women who had offered us hospitality he and she hurrying both of them grasping black bags in a large trash can he's dragging along an old half-open suitcase upholstered in checkered fabric—

the dignity of this look—

II

it was upon returning from the flower market suddenly at the corner of the dock and the footbridge to île Saint-Louis under the high windows where the shadow of Jankélévitch and Edmond Fleg flits by this Balkan melody on his accordion time just enough time to exchange a few words about this place and his country and when it's too cold this burning coffee he clasps in both hands he says, he shares a cellar, and also, no, not a place for flowers, and he almost laughs, and takes up the Balkan melody again—

de ces beautés qui font le monde habitable

oui tu as raison elle était jolie la maison quand j'étais petite je voudrais te la raconter elle est au bout d'un grand voyage dans une rue en pente sur la Colline des Roses – Rószadomb – et tout en bas le Danube comme une coulée de lumière après une petite enfance sur les routes d'exode. Ma vraie maison. Je veux dire là où tu te sais attendu accueilli. Comme pour toujours. Havre de beauté la nappe bleue ajourée à la main bleu-douceur qui n'existe nulle part ailleurs l'arôme d'une soupe à l'aneth les fleurs fraîches dans le vase en terre –

de ces beautés qui font le monde habitable –

of these beauties that make the world habitable

yes you're right it was pretty my house when I was little I would like to tell you it is at the end of a long trip down a steep street on the Rose Hill—Rószadomb—and at the very bottom the Danube like a stream of light after an early childhood on the roads of exodus. My true house. I mean where you expect to be welcomed. Always. Haven of beauty the blue hand-sewn tablecloth softness-blue which doesn't exist anywhere else the aroma of a dill soup fresh flowers in an earthen vase—

of these beauties that make the world habitable—

une maison intérieure

intonations du hongrois mélanges des parlers là-bas au versant du Danube tu auras appris pour la vie : habiter une maison intérieure toute de voix qui t'enchantent –

et de mots qui parlent une langue d'âme –

an interior house

intonations of Hungarian mixtures of dialects over there on the side of the Danube you will have learned for life: to fully inhabit an interior house filled with voices which enchant you—

and with words which speak a soul language—

maison nomade

I

dans ton souvenir ce premier train pour Budapest longe un torrent couleur des glaciers je ne savais pas encore que c'était l'Inn descendue de l'Engadine et que bien des années plus tard je la retrouverais au confluent du Danube et de l'Ilz. À Passau. Où, un jour, le poète Reiner Kunze trouvera refuge à quelques kilomètres en aval. Et là au croisement des traces du passé où déjà s'inscrivent les traces à venir j'apprendrai à habiter le lent passage des mots et des poèmes –

maison nomade le long des eaux vives –

II

dans la maison de Reiner Kunze. Ce soir de fin mars 2016. Sur le jardin en pente, la nuit tombe entre l'or des forsythias et les traces de la dernière neige. Dans nos verres, un vin de Croatie. Fruité et sombre. La meilleure bouteille du poète. Il se prépare aux rencontres et lectures en Ukraine pour la parution du volume de ses poèmes aux éditions Knyhy à Tchernivtsi (l'ancienne Czernowitz). Dans cette lumière du crépuscule, je songe à ses poèmes des années d'exil dans son propre pays. Interdit de lectures et publications, exclu de la chambre des écrivains de RDA. Oui, ces mêmes poèmes, traduits aujourd'hui en ukrainien et qu'il va présenter à Kiev et Czernowitz

nomadic house

I

in your memory this first train for Budapest along a torrent the color of glaciers I did not know yet that it was the Inn coming down from the Engadine and that many years later I would find it again at the junction of the Danube and the Ilz. At Passau. Where, one day, the poet Reiner Kunze will find refuge a few kilometers downstream. And there at the crossroads traces of the past where traces to come are already inscribed I will learn to inhabit the slow passage of words and poems—

nomadic house along the white waters—

II

in the house of Reiner Kunze. This evening in late March 2016. On the sloping garden, night falls between the gold of forsythias and traces of the last snow. In our glasses, a Croatian wine. Fruited and dark. The poet's best bottle. He prepares himself for meetings and readings in Ukraine for the publication of a volume of his poems in the Knyhy editions at Tchernivitsi (formerly Czernowitz). In the dusky light of the setting sun, I dream of his poems, of the years of exile in his own country. Forbidden from readings and publications, excluded from the writers' room of the GDR. Yes, these same poems, translated today into Ukrainian, that he's going to present at Kiev and Czernowitz

Même quand il s'abat
l'arbre dans l'arbre ne meurt
que lentement

ainsi de l'humain dans l'homme

écrit deux ans avant l'écrasement du Printemps de Prague par les troupes soviétiques –

Czernowitz, ville aux marges et confins de l'empire austro-hongrois : Galicie Roumanie Bessarabie Ukraine. Creuset de tant de langues et cultures : yiddish allemand ukrainien russe roumain ruthène –
Czernowitz, tant de penseurs et de savants, de poètes et d'écrivains déportés, exilés, assassinés. Tant de parlers métissés et intimes, tant d'êtres « déclarés comme Néant » (Imre Kertész) –

il y eut ce jour à Genève, cher Jean Halpérin, nous parlions du poème de Celan, *Psalm-Psaume*. Et du mot « niemand » et vous me disiez que le mot allemand, comme le mot hébreu correspondant, est un absolu d'absence, de négation, et ne comporte pas l'ambiguïté du mot français « personne ». C'est l'homme-réduit-à-néant. Et nous avons choisi de le traduire par « l'homme-néantisé » : *niht-man* :

C'est l'homme-néantisé qui nous pétrira de nouveau
   de terre et d'argile
l'homme-néantisé qui donnera parole à notre
   poussière

anéantissement de l'humain auquel Imre Kertész oppose un même « ethos de la résistance » –

Even when it falls
the tree inside the tree
only dies slowly

so it is with humanity in man

written two years before the Soviet troops crushed the Prague Spring—

Czernowitz, city at the margins and confines of the Austro-Hungarian empire: Galicia Romania Bessarabia Ukraine. Source of so many languages and cultures: Yiddish German Ukrainian Russian Romanian Ruthenian— Czernowitz, so many thinkers and scientists, poets and writers deported, exiled, assassinated. So many mixed and intimate dialects, so many beings "declared as Nothingness" (Imre Kertész)—

there was one day in Geneva, dear Jean Halpérin, we were talking about Celan's poem, *Psalm-Psaume*. And about the word "niemand" and you were telling me that the German word, like the Hebrew equivalent, is an absolute absence, negation, and doesn't include the ambiguity of the French word "person." It is man-reduced-to-nothingness. And we chose to translate it as "no-man": *niht-man*:

> *It is the no-man who will knead us again from*
> > *earth and clay*
> *the no-man who will give voice to our dust*

annihilation of the human to which Imre Kertész opposes a similar "ethos of resistance"—

du choix de cette traduction de *niemand,* Marc Faessler nous écrira : « Elle fait se rejoindre Paul Celan, Nelly Sachs et Rilke. C'est cela le retournement de la langue pour faire échec à son usage par les bourreaux. Force de la Parole dans le langage de la langue ! » –
et en ce soir de mars 2016, comme à voix basse et grave, Reiner Kunze lit *Psalm* de Paul Celan puis il ajoute : « Siehst du, *blühend* – blühen, das Schöne das Leben trotz alledem » – « Tu vois, *fleurissant* – fleurir, le beau la vie envers et contre tout » –

cette nuit-là, tandis que je redescendais la rue, il y avait sous les étoiles, plus forts que le vent glacial qui soufflait du fleuve, ces poèmes migrants de toutes les langues, ces paroles de passeurs qu'aucune frontière ne pourra arrêter –

en bas, au bord du Danube, stationnés sur le parking du petit hôtel, trois cars loués à des compagnies de tourisme par la police des frontières –

sur l'autre rive, c'est l'Autriche –

III

Voici le soleil plus bas, la Néva plus brumeuse
Et l'espoir nous chante au loin, au loin.
...
Que s'en aillent sur la Néva en silence les bateaux

Requiem. Tu m'as offert ce livre. Il y a bien des années. Dans une petite édition qu'on emporte sur toutes les routes. C'est

after choosing this translation of *niemand*, Marc Faessler writes us: "It brings together Paul Celan, Nelly Sachs and Rilke. This is the reversal of language to prevent its usage by the executioners. The Power of Words in the tongue's language!"—
and this evening of March 2016, with a low and serious voice, Reiner Kunze reads Paul Celan's *Psalm*: then he adds: «*Siehst du, blühend—blühen, das Schöne das Leben trotz alledem*»—"You see, *blooming*—to bloom, the beautiful life against all odds"—

that night, while I was coming down the street, there were under the stars, stronger than the glacial wind blowing in from the river, these migrant poems from all languages, these smuggled words no border can stop—

below, at the edge of the Danube, stationed in the parking lot of the little hotel, three cars
rented from tourist companies by the border police—

on the other shore, Austria—

III

Here the sun is lower, the Neva mistier
And hope sings to us in the distance, in the distance.
...
Let the boats on the Neva go in silence

Requiem. You gave me this book. Many years ago. In a small edition I carry with me wherever I go. It is with these verses

avec ces vers que j'ai découvert Anna Akhmatova depuis je les habite comme une de ces maisons dont on dit qu'elles ont une âme –

that I discovered Anna Akhmatova ever since I've lived in
them like one of those houses they say has a soul—

une maison vers là-bas

quand la petite fille a quitté la famille de Budapest elle a dessiné un train et le long du train un cours d'eau bleu. Et des fleurs. Et un quai désert. Et depuis tu sais que l'attente est un pays secret un pays de silence et que l'absence est une manière d'espérer. Peut-être vient-il de là ce penchant pour retrouver les objets perdus. Et aussi pour les mots qui traduisent. Et si traduire c'était chercher des mots perdus ?

oui, un dessin. Comme une lettre. Comme une maison perdue. Une maison vers là-bas –

a house over there

when the little girl left the Budapest family she drew a train and along the train a current of blue water. And flowers. And a deserted platform. And since you've known that waiting is a secret country a country of silence and that absence is a manner of hoping. Perhaps from that comes this penchant for finding lost things again. And also for the words that translate. And what if to translate was to look for lost words?

yes, a drawing. Like a letter. Like a lost house. A house over there—

ne pas laisser de traces

quel mot saura dire cette maison-enfance ? emportée dans un train de nuit parti de Budapest Keleti. Maison natale comme on dit de nos langues natales. Où venir au monde. Et à soi-même. Ce mot je l'ai découvert à Londres chez un fin lettré dans une maison toute de livres. Il se trouve dans les *Passages* que Walter Benjamin acheva d'écrire pendant son exil à Paris. C'était en 1934. Sous la grande verrière de la Bibliothèque nationale. Il dit une maison – *Gehäuse* – : « où s'abriter. Trouver refuge ». Parfois sur les routes d'errance en certains lieux tu découvriras de ces traces « qui réorganisent l'espace à travers lui le temps » –

elles te ramèneront vers cette maison emportée « où habiter sans laisser de traces » –

leave no trace

what word could express this childhood home? swept away on a night train from Budapest Keleti. Motherland as we say of our mother tongue. Where to arrive in the world. And in oneself. This word I discovered in London in the house of a man of letters that was filled with books. It is in *Passages* that Walter Benjamin finished writing during his exile in Paris. It was in 1934. Below the large stained-glass window of the Bibliothèque nationale. He calls a house—*Gehäuse*: "where one takes shelter. Finds refuge." Sometimes along the more meandering roads you will discover traces "reorganizing space and through it time."

they will bring you to this swept away house "where to live leaving no trace"—

au partage des eaux

ainsi de ces lieux frontières. Au partage des eaux. Des rêves et des mémoires. À l'angle du quai près du pont du Rhône où les eaux encore sauvages du fleuve sortent du lac. Cette plaque de bronze apposée au parapet 10 septembre 1898 l'impératrice Élisabeth reine de Hongrie assassinée près de l'embarcadère fine silhouette femme-fleur de pierre à ses pieds une rose posée quelque bouquet discret à deux pas de là un panneau explique les oiseaux des eaux et des roselières. Impératrice poète. Après le suicide de son fils Rodolphe et sa bien-aimée Marie Vetsera elle ne porta plus que du noir renonça à la poésie et confia ses poèmes au président de la confédération à Berne avec pour consigne de ne les publier qu'en 1950 au profit des prisonniers politiques. Elle appelait Heine son maître et devant le refus de Dusseldorf la ville natale du poète de lui ériger une statue sur son sol elle en réalisa une dans les jardins de son château privé à Corfou –

une plaque de bronze apposée sur les eaux. Comme sur une maison. Engloutie –

to the parting of the waters

and so these border places. To the parting of the waters. Dreams and memories. At the corner of the dock near the bridge of the Rhône where wild river waters leave the lake. Affixed to the parapet this bronze plaque 10 September 1898 the Empress Elisabeth Queen of Hungary assassinated near the pier a thin stone a woman-flower silhouette a rose at her feet a discreet bouquet close by a sign describing water birds and rose beds. Empress poet. Always in black after her son Rodolphe and his beloved Marie Vetsera's suicides. She renounced poetry, confided her poems to the president of the confederation in Berne with instructions not to publish until 1950 to benefit political prisoners. Called Heine her teacher. When Dusseldorf the poet's birthplace refused to erect his statue she had one created for the gardens of her private castle in Corfu—

a bronze plaque affixed above the waters. Like on a house. Engulfed—

mu'allaqāt

combien de poètes avant moi ! est-il encore des chants inchantés ?
te souviens-tu, mon âme triste, où fut sa tente ?

...

plein de doutes, je me suis arrêté dans les pâturages cherchant
   les traces de ses chameaux

...

là sur le sable, les pierres du foyer, noires dans leur vide –

Imrû'l-Qays (env. 550)

mu'allaqāt: the hanging odes

how many singers before me? are there still songs unsung?
do you remember, my sad soul, where was his tent?

...

full of doubts, I stopped in pastures, seeking the trace of his camels

...

there on the sand, the hearth-stones, black in their emptiness—

—Imru' al-Qays (approx. 550 CE)

maison des mots

> *les mots sont la matière première*
> *pour construire une maison –*
> **Mahmoud Darwich**

ce fut un ou deux hivers après Budapest désormais inscrite au cadran du temps et des géographies du cœur peut-être une leçon à apprendre pour l'école puisque *Oceano nox* se trouvait dans une édition scolaire toujours est-il que ce fut un instant foudroyant l'irruption de la poésie dans une vie mais qu'est-ce qu'une enfant de dix ans pouvait bien entendre dans ces vers ? peut-être la réponse est-elle dans ces minuscules croix comme autant de petites étoiles à l'encre violette que ta main d'enfant a tracées au premier et au dernier mot de quelques vers

Nul ne saura leur fin dans l'abîme plongée
(...)
Nul ne sait votre sort pauvres têtes perdues
(...)
Oh, que de vieux parents, qui n'avaient plus qu'un rêve,
Sont morts en attendant tous les jours sur la grève
        Ceux qui ne sont pas revenus !...

peut-être quelque mystérieuse résonance avec ce grand voyage parmi les survivants de la famille –

le poème comme une maison d'âme où une voix a chanté pour toi et parlé tout bas là où il y avait les silences de trop de douleur –

house of words

> *words are raw materials for*
> *building a house—*
> **Mahmoud Darwish**

it happened here one or two winters after Budapest henceforth inscribed on the dial of time and geographies of the heart perhaps a lesson to learn during schooltime since *Oceano nox* could be found in a scholarly edition the fact remains it was a moment of lightning the irruption of poetry in a life but what could a ten-year-old hear in these verses? the answer may lie in these tiny crosses like so many little stars that your child's hand traced in purple ink on the first and last word

No one will know their end in the deep abyss
(...)
No one knows your fate poor lost heads
(...)

Oh, those old parents, who had only one dream left, died while waiting every day on the pebble beach
        Those who didn't return!...

perhaps some mysterious resonance of this great voyage among survivors of the family—

the poem like a soul house where a voice sang for you and spoke softly where there were silences of too much pain—

des mots comme un refuge

> Non loin d'une montagne escarpée qu'on appelle le Pas-de-l'Échelle, au-dessous du grand chemin taillé dans le roc à l'endroit appelé Chailles, court et bouillonne dans des gouffres affreux une petite rivière qui paraît avoir mis à les creuser des milliers de siècles. On a bordé le chemin d'un parapet pour prévenir les malheurs : cela faisait que je pouvais contempler au fond et gagner des vertiges tout à mon aise...
>
> J.-J. Rousseau, *Les Confessions*

après l'hiver après le retour il y eut ces étés on arrêtait les vélos au sommet de la route au lieu-dit Chailles et c'était comme un rite de grimper au promontoire au-dessus des gorges du Guiers. Avant de prendre le sentier escarpé on passait devant deux panneaux en bois sur l'un on voyait un bonhomme emporté par les éboulements de ces roches du massif de Chartreuse sur l'autre il y avait un texte aux couleurs des intempéries je relisais tout bas chaque fois ses mots qui disaient mon effroi muet. Des mots à hauteur d'un cœur d'enfant devant le vide –

des mots comme un refuge –

words as shelter

> *A short distance from a craggy mountain we call le Pas-de-l'Échelle, below a wide road carved out in the bedrock at the spot called Chailles, runs and bubbles in the frightful chasms a small river which seems to have spent thousands of centuries carving them. The path is lined with a parapet in order to prevent misfortunes: hence I could contemplate the bottom and experience vertigos all at my leisure...*
> Jean-Jacques Rousseau, *Les Confessions*

after the winter after the return there were these summers we stopped our bicycles at the summit of the road at Chailles and it was like a ritual to climb to the promontory above the gorges of Guiers. Before taking the steep path we passed in front of two wooden boards on one we saw a newspaper clipping of a man carried away by the landslides of these rocks of the Chartreuse mountain range on the other there was a text in the colors of bad weather I reread softly every time these words which spoke my mute terror. Words the height of a child's heart in front of the void—

words as shelter—

comme autant de petites maisons où apprendre à habiter le monde

c'était un soir de neige sur Silbertal. Réuni autour de la table le comité d'Histoire du village. Vous cherchez : comment réaliser une exposition pour faire connaître reconnaître Eugénie Goldstern ? cette ethnologue du premier quart du vingtième siècle qui arpenta vos vallées. Déportée de Vienne. Exterminée à Sobibor. Et votre question lancinante : mais comment parler de Sobibor ? dans cette nuit glaciale cela s'imposa soudain : transmettre la part de lumière et de vie. Son amour de la maison et à travers elle des habitants de vos vallées. Et les plus reculées. Elle qui n'avait pas de maison elle sauva la mémoire de vos maisons. Elle a noté, décrit, dessiné, photographié tout ce qui en faisait un abri. Tout ce qui en faisait la beauté. Avec la même humble ferveur elle collecta, cœur secret de vos maisons, les jouets, les premiers de la terre, taillés dans des branchettes, des os, des coques de fruits, dépositaires des rêves et des peurs des enfants –

comme autant de petites maisons où apprendre à habiter le monde –

like so many little houses where one learns to inhabit the world

it was a snowy night at Silbertal. Gathered around the table the committee of the History of the village. You search: how to set up an exposition to introduce to recognize Eugénie Goldstern? this ethnographer of the first quarter of the twentieth century who surveyed your valleys. Deported from Vienna. Exterminated at Sobibor. And your piercing question: but how to speak of Sobibor? in this glacial night it imposes itself suddenly: to transmit the part of light and of life. Her love for the house and through it the inhabitants of your valleys. And the most remote. She who had no house she saved the memory of your houses. She noted, described, sketched, photographed everything that made them a shelter. All that made their beauty. With the same humble fervor she collected, secret heart of your houses, the toys, the firsts of the earth, carved from twigs, bones, shells of fruit, repository of children's dreams and fears—

like so many little houses where one learns to inhabit the world—

maison arc-en-ciel

sur le quai. La foule. Et ton amie Lou. Vous avez encore tout juste huit ans. Le train est annoncé. Vous vous serrez très fort dans vos bras comme pour un grand voyage tous les départs sont un grand voyage et il y a du soleil sur la petite table près de la fenêtre et tu sors ton petit carnet et le crayon noir et lentement soigneusement tu vous dessines et puis tu choisis tes crayons de couleur tu commences par vos yeux Lou a tes yeux verts et les tiens sont brun doré et tu as retrouvé ton sourire et vous avez des habits préférés –

et ils ont les couleurs de l'arc-en-ciel –

rainbow house

on the dock. The crowd. And your friend Lou. And you are still just eight years old. The train is announced. You hug each other very hard as though for a great voyage all departures are a great voyage and there is sun on the little table near the window and you take out your little notebook and black pencil and slowly carefully you draw and then you choose the colored pencils and you begin with your eyes Lou has green eyes and yours are golden brown and you found your smile and you have your favorite clothes—

and they are the colors of the rainbow—

petites baraques foraines

I

la petite fille marchait dans le soir elle tenait dans ses bras un grand poisson aux écailles d'or. Un poisson articulé avec des morceaux de chambre à air noirs et rigides comme celles des sandales des maquisards du Viet Bac qu'on appelait sandales Ho Chi Minh. C'était pourtant d'autres temps. Mais elles viennent de si loin dans les paysages humains ces marionnettes du Vietnam. Et ce soir dans les bras de la petite fille tout au bout de la ville aux confluences du Rhône et de la Saône un poisson aux écailles d'or comme échappé de la troupe. Un poisson en bois avec deux trous pour les tiges de bambou et le marionnettiste pieds nus dans les rizières les fait glisser à fleur d'eau parmi les lotus et le poisson aux écailles d'or a bondi et dansé. Terre ou eau. Poisson des fonds marins de la petite sirène dans le conte d'Andersen. Petit poisson d'or du vieux pêcheur et de sa femme rapace dans le conte russe. Petit poisson d'or qui va sauver Tam « Brisure de riz » petite sœur vietnamienne de Cendrillon deux noms de très loin pour une même misère où est la terre où est l'eau ?

en émerveille plus loin que les mots –

small fairground stalls

I

a little girl was walking in the evening she held in her hands a big fish with golden scales. A fish joined with pieces of an inner tube black and rigid like those sandals of the *maquisards* of Viet Bac that were called Ho Chi Minh sandals. That was another time. But they come from so far away in the human landscapes these puppets from Vietnam. And this evening in the arms of the little girl at the very end of the city at the junction of the Rhône and Saône a fish with golden scales as if escaped from its school. A wooden fish with two holes for the bamboo stems and the puppeteer barefoot in the rice fields slides them on the surface of the water among the lotus and the fish with golden scales jumped and danced. Earth or water. Fish of the seabed of the little mermaid in Andersen's tale. Little fish of gold of the old fisherman and his greedy wife in the Russian story. Little fish of gold going to rescue Tam "Rice Breakage" Cinderella's little Vietnamese sister two names from far away in the same misery where is the earth where is the water?

in wonder further away than words—

II

le marchand de marionnettes
Goya (1793)
peint sur fer-blanc –
« afin d'occuper mon imagination mortifiée
par la considération de mes maux »
maladie surdité Terreur guerres

ce qui fait la nuit en nous
peut laisser en nous les étoiles
Victor Hugo, *Quatre-vingt-treize*

cette lumière de fin d'été sur le lac et les montagnes tu es d'accord pour venir voir ce tableau juste ce tableau et tu me diras j'ai besoin de ton regard d'enfant alors on a pris la descente le long du Collège Calvin et de ton pas dansant tu as gravi le majestueux escalier du musée c'était juste avant la fermeture et tu as trouvé la salle 18 tu verras c'est le premier tableau sur ta gauche

> *je ne voudrais pas être dans ce paysage, il est triste*
> et rassurée tu as ajouté
> *mais les enfants, ils sont bien*

oui, ils sont là en arc de cercle le visage éclairé par la lueur des minuscules marionnettes le regard captivé par le petit montreur pieds nus en haillons caché dans la grande cape en lambeaux du marchand. Il est si petit on ne voit pas leurs yeux on ne voit que leurs paupières baissées vers lui –

on ne voit que leurs rêves –

II

> *the puppet seller*
> *Goya (1793)*
> *painted on white iron*
> *"in order to occupy my mortified imagination by the consideration of my ills"*
> *illness deafness war Terrors*
>
> *that which makes the night in us*
> *could leave in us the stars*
> **Victor Hugo,** *Ninety-Three*

this light of late summer on the lake and the mountains you agree to come see this painting just this painting and you will tell me I need your childish look then we walked downhill along Collège Calvin and in your dancing steps you climbed the majestic staircase of the museum it was just before closing and you found room 18 you will see it is the first painting on your left

> *I would not want to be in this landscape, it is sad*
> and reassured you added
> *but the children, they are well*

yes, they are there in an arc their faces lit by the glow of the tiny puppets their gazes captivated by the little barefoot showman in rags hidden in the merchant's large tattered cape. He is so small we only see their eyes we only see their eyelids lowered toward him—

we only see their dreams—

III

beauty is the spirit of all things
Charlie Chaplin

apprendre une ville par la main d'un enfant dévaler les pentes de la Croix-Rousse depuis votre petite école au bord de l'amphithéâtre romain jusqu'au vieux cinéma d'art et d'essai et là, avec la volée de moineaux de votre classe bien calés dans les fauteuils de velours, soudain attendu préparé depuis des semaines Charlot et de plain-pied cette complicité du rire et jusqu'au bord des larmes comme un ami à mille lieues des mots et quand le petit bonhomme s'en est allé tout seul au fond de l'écran vous l'avez encore accompagné et son silence et votre silence loin si loin du monde assourdissant. Et un jour l'ami afghan notre chauffeur de taxi, à nous Princes sans voiture, il t'a raconté sa découverte du petit homme au chapeau melon, c'était à Kaboul, il avait quatorze ou quinze ans, avant les désastres guerres et exils un ami l'avait emmené au centre culturel américain ce fut son premier film de Charlot et depuis c'est son compagnon et avec ses mots afghans il t'a dit en français « *Charlot, c'est comme un proverbe ramassé, une philosophie* » et il a serré ta petite main –

comme un pacte par-delà les paroles et toutes les frontières –

III

beauty is the spirit of all things
Charlie Chaplin

to learn a city by the hand of a child is to race down the slopes of la Croix-Rousse since your little school borders the Roman amphitheater up to the old art house cinema and there, the flock of sparrows that is your class in the velour seats, suddenly awaited prepared for weeks Charlot straight to the point on one level this complicity of laughter and up to the verge of tears like a friend a thousand leagues of words away and when the little guy went all by himself to the bottom of the screen you accompanied him again and his silence and your silence far away so far from the deafening world. And one day an Afghan friend our taxi driver, to us carless princes, he told you his discovery of the little man with a bowler hat, it was in Kabul, he was fourteen or fifteen, before the disastrous wars and exiles a friend had led him to the American Cultural Center it was his first Charlot film and since then he has been his companion and with his Afghan words he said to you in French *"Charlot, it's like a collected proverb, a philosophy"* and he squeezed your little hand—

like a pact beyond words and borders—

un abri où déposer un mot d'âme

Ce n'est qu'avec toi, étranger,
que je puis parler ma langue
car toi aussi tu viens de loin
    Lalla Romano

c'était un matin de fin d'automne et cette femme montée à Genève avec cette énorme valise à caser le train longe le lac elle arrive du Brésil. En mettant bout à bout ses bribes d'anglais. De français. Un peu d'allemand. Elle va jusqu'à Lausanne. Une amie doit l'héberger. Elle espère un travail. Et voit la neige. C'est la première fois. Un long silence. Et soudain. Un mot. Comme lancé sur les eaux :
saudade
elle le répète en ricochets :
    – *saudade,* on ne peut pas traduire
elle essaye : « mélancolie longing nostalgie sehnsucht... ».
Comme si elle cherchait un abri où déposer ce mot d'âme. Qu'il soit accueilli justement dans son étrangeté. Alors, comme si seule la musique savait cela, elle dit que *saudade* c'est comme le Fado. Et elle dit aussi : écoute Cesária Évora sa chanson *Sodade* dans sa voix tu entends tout. Elle est descendue avec son énorme valise –

elle était seule sur le quai –

a shelter to deposit a soul's word

> *It is only with you, stranger,*
> *that I can speak my language*
> *because you also come from afar*
> **Lalla Romano**

it was a late autumn morning and this woman boarded at Geneva with an enormous suitcase to cram in the train goes along the lake she arrives from Brazil. By putting bits and pieces of English together. Of French. A little German. She goes all the way to Lausanne. A friend is supposed to lodge her. She hopes for work. And sees the snow. It's the first time. A long silence.
And suddenly. A word. Like tossed to the waters:
saudade
she repeats it in ricochets:
　　—*saudade*, one can't translate it
she tries: "melancholy longing nostalgia *sehnsucht*..." As if she were searching for a shelter where to put this soul's word. May it be welcomed in its strangeness. Then, as if only music understood it, she says *saudade* is like the Fado. And she also says: listen to Cesária Évora her song *Sodade* in her voice you hear everything. She descended with her enormous suitcase—

she was alone on the platform—

comme une maison de vent

appel immémorial aux accents des Balkans les gens sont sortis de leurs immeubles pour écouter c'était hier matin sur la place déserte dans ce silence de la mi-août un homme assis sur le muret à ses pieds un morceau de carton tracé en lettres exilées du cyrillique

                Korna Mus
                Bulgari

dans ses bras rude et blanche une peau de mouton souffle et enfle un chant de berger errant –

comme une maison de vent –

like a house of wind

immemorial summons to the voices of the Balkans the people went out of their apartment buildings to listen it was yesterday morning on the deserted square in this silence of mid-August a man seated on the low wall at his feet a scrap of cardboard traced with exiled letters from Cyrillic
          Korna Mus
          Bulgari
in his hands rough and white a sheepskin blows and puffs out a song of a wandering shepherd—

like a house of wind—

rendre un mot habitable

mille fois plus natale...
la terre où tout est libre et fraternel,
ma terre.
                Aimé Césaire

comme une lettre à Bruno Winkler
historien et éducateur à Montafon, dans le Vorarlberg

ce matin d'hiver. Le village de Schruns de la commune de Montafon. Montagnes alentour et rues étroites tout était sous la haute neige. Et jusqu'à la petite place où se trouve le musée. *Heimatmuseum* : comment traduire ce mot ? et déjà *Heimat* ? le pays natal et la maison, *home*, le chez-soi. Un mot où il y a de l'intime : peut-être parce qu'au moyen-âge l'accent fort était mis sur la voyelle qui précède le « t », et se prononçait « ô » créant ainsi un malentendu avec *Mut*. Un mot où se dit un état d'âme.

Heimat oscille entre l'intime et le collectif, entre le spirituel et le terrestre. Un mot « sensible », comme il en est dans chaque langue, marqué au sceau d'une Histoire. Ainsi dans la langue allemande forgée dans le creuset spirituel, moral, politique de la traduction que Luther fit de la Bible.

Oui, comment traduire aujourd'hui : Heimatmuseum ? Et d'abord, comment l'entendre ? Sans doute en prenant en compte les strates de l'Histoire déposées dans le mot Heimat et cette institution muséale assujettis par le nazisme. Peut-être aussi en se rendant sur place. En prenant le pouls. Sur le terrain.

Tu m'avais prévenue : « Des Heimatmuseum, dans la vallée, il y en a trois. Mais tu verras, dans ce microcosme de migrations à l'échelle mondiale qu'est la vallée de Montafon, notre

to make a word habitable

> *a thousand times more native...*
> *the earth where all is free and fraternal*
> *my earth*
> Aimé Césaire

like a letter to Bruno Winkler
historian and educator at Montafon in the Vorarlberg

this winter morning. The village of Schruns of the municipality of Montafon. Surrounding mountains and narrow streets all buried in high snow. And up to the small square where one finds the museum. *Heimatmuseum*: how to translate this word? and then *Heimat*? The native country and the house, *home*, the home. A word where there is intimacy: perhaps because in the Middle Ages the strong accent was put on the vowel that preceded the "t," and was pronounced "o," thus creating a misunderstanding with *Mut*. A word that speaks of a state of mind.

Heimat oscillates between the intimate and the collective, between the spiritual and the terrestrial. A "sensitive" word of the sort that exists in every language, marked with the stamp of a History. And so in the German language forged in the spiritual, moral, political hearth of the translation Luther made of the Bible.

Yes, how to translate today: Heimatmuseum? And first, how to understand it? Doubtless by taking into account the layers of history deposited in the word Heimat and this museum subjugated by Nazism. Perhaps also by on-the-spot visits. Taking the pulse. In the field.

You warned me: "Heimatmuseums, in the valley, there are three. But you will see, in this microcosm of global migrations,

musée est atypique– *unüblich*. » Et quand je t'ai demandé pourquoi vous lui avez gardé ce nom, tu as ajouté : « C'est vrai, le concept de Heimat-Heimatmuseum a été perverti de la pire manière dans le passé et l'est encore aujourd'hui par une idéologie de l'exclusion de "l'autre", des "autres". Mais pour nous, Heimat doit devenir synonyme de pays d'accueil, et le musée, le Heimatmuseum, lui aussi doit prendre sa part dans ce pays d'accueil. Dans la vallée de Montafon. Et justement aussi à Schruns où sont hébergés dans le Foyer Caritas Santa Rast et chez des habitants, des réfugiés d'Afghanistan, Iran, Liban, Syrie, Irak, Azerbaïdjan, Arménie, Érythrée, Albanie, Égypte, Ukraine, du Pakistan, Sénégal, Congo, Kosovo, Daguestan, Sri Lanka, de Géorgie, Tchétchénie, Syrie, Somalie, Mongolie. Pour relever ce défi, notre Heimatmuseum s'est positionné dans la vallée comme médiateur, modérateur dans les dissensions, affrontements, prises de position et décisions liés à cette *"brisante Präsenz"* des demandeurs d'asile. » Comme elle est éloquente ton expression : « *brisante Präsenz* » ! Ces deux mots d'origine étrangère accentuent le poids de cette « présence » et la « brisure » des êtres sur les routes de l'exil, les « fractures » parmi les habitants de la commune.

Oui, la neige était haute. Le vent glacial. Mais il y eut votre accueil si chaleureux autour de la table et ce bon café de l'amitié tandis que tu racontes ton initiative soutenue par le directeur du musée, Andreas Rudigier, et toute l'équipe, et accompagnée par des bénévoles du village et des environs et par une jeune artiste de Schruns, Rebecca Marent, aidée par des amies étudiantes aux Beaux-Arts de Brême.

Oui, le vent est glacial. Mais comme elle rayonne, cette autre chaleur : le long des vitrines et voisinant avec les objets usuels des gens de la vallée et de leur artisanat, et ceux des bergers et de la vie pastorale et des alpages, et ces documents sur les refuges, lieux de survie et de passage le long de ces

which is the valley of Montafon, our museum is atypical—*unüblich.*" And when I asked you why you have kept this name, you added: "It's true, the concept of Heimat-Heimatmuseum has been perverted in the worst possible way in the past and still today by an ideology of exclusion of 'the other,' of 'the others.' But for us, Heimat ought to become synonymous of a welcoming country, and the museum, Heimatmuseum, also ought to take its part in this welcoming country. In the valley of Montafon. And rightly so at Schruns where they are lodged in the Foyer Caritas Santa Rast and in inhabitants' homes, the refugees from Afghanistan, Iran, Libya, Syria, Iraq, Azerbaijan, Armenia, Eritrea, Albania, Egypt, Ukraine, from Pakistan, Senegal, Congo, Kosovo, Dagestan, Sri Lanka, Georgia, Chechnya, Somalia, Mongolia. In order to take up this challenge, our Heimatmuseum set itself up in the valley as a mediator, moderator in the dissensions, clashes, positions taken, tied to this *"brisante Präsenz"* of the asylum seekers. How eloquent is your expression *"brisante Präsenz!"* These two words of foreign origin accentuate the weight of this "presence" and the "fragmentation" of people on the roads of exile, the "fractures" among the inhabitants of the commune. Yes, the snow was high. The wind glacial. But there was your welcome so warm around the table and this good coffee of friendship while you talk about your initiative supported by the museum director, Andreas Rudigier, and the whole team, and accompanied by volunteers of the village and surrounding areas and by a young artist of Schruns, Rebecca Marent, helped by student friends at Les Beaux-Arts de Brême.

Yes, the wind is glacial. But how it radiates, this other warmth: along the windows and neighboring everyday objects by people of the valley and their crafts, and those of the shepherds and of pastoral life and high mountain pastures, and these documents about the shelters, places of survival and of

crêtes frontalières, placés sous haute surveillance des nazis dès l'Anschluss puis rapidement interdits d'accès et fermés.

Oui, voisinent ainsi ces fresques peintes par des réfugiés de Somalie, d'Érythrée, du Sénégal : grands panneaux aux couleurs rouge pour dire le pays, le désert, et bleu pour la mer, et entre, les poissons noirs, pour leur travail comme pêcheurs sur la côte, et à gauche et à droite, consciemment en marge de tout le tableau, il y a l'Europe l'Autriche Schruns. Ils sont arrivés et vivent. Mais encore en marge.

Et près d'une ancienne affiche du Heimatmuseum, un autre tableau. Les couleurs rappellent le désert, le soleil (rouge et jaune) et une petite oasis (vert). Et les lignes noires sont des frontières. Et complètement à droite dans le tableau, une série de silhouettes, des réfugiés en route.

Oui, voisinant : les humbles objets témoins des migrations qui firent, au long des siècles, l'histoire de ces vallées, migrations de misère et de survie : muletiers, enfants saisonniers venus de Souabe, coupeurs de choux, moissonneurs, vagues migratoires d'Alsaciens, de Walser, de Lombards.

Sous ces mêmes plafonds, le long de ces mêmes murs, sous ce même toit, un groupe de musiciens du Kenya et Congo avec un garçonnet d'Arménie, et un jeune de Schruns s'exerce avec eux au djembé, ils vont former un petit orchestre qui jouera pour l'inauguration de l'exposition dans la salle Montafon du Musée. Ils répètent sur un fond de statues d'angelots, et de Vierges Marie auréolées et dorées et comme échappées d'une chapelle baroque.

Tu me montres ces photos d'un groupe d'art-thérapie : devant un cerisier en fleurs des femmes et une enfant de Mongolie ont présenté en public une danse avec de longs voiles blancs qu'elles ont confectionnés avec des femmes du village.

Dans une salle où sont accrochées des séries de coucous contre une paroi de sapin, une femme de Mongolie, la bouche

crossing along these border ridges, places under high surveillance by the Nazis since Anschluss then rapidly forbidden to access then closed. Yes, these frescoes adjoin those painted by refugees from Somalia, Eritrea, Senegal: large colored panels red to tell the country, the desert, blue for the sea, and in between, black fish, for their work as fishermen on the coast, and from left to right, consciously on the fringe of the whole picture, there's Europe Austria Schruns. They arrived and are living. But still on the margin.

And near an old poster of the Heimatmuseum, another painting. The colors recall the desert, the sun (red and yellow) and a small oasis (green). And the black lines are the borders. And all the way to the right of the painting, a series of silhouettes, refugees on route.

Yes, neighbors: humble objects, witnesses of migrations, made throughout the centuries, the history of these valleys, migrations of misery and survival: muleteers, seasonal children from Swabia, cabbage cutters, harvesters, migratory waves of Alsatians, of Walsers, of Lombards.

Under these same ceilings, along these same walls, under this same roof, a group of musicians from Kenya and Congo with a young boy from Armenia, and a youth from Schruns practices with them on the djembe, they want to form a small orchestra which will play at the inauguration of the exposition in the Montafon room of the Museum. They practice at the foot of cherub statues, and Virgin Marys haloed and gilded as if escapees from a baroque chapel.

You show me these photos of an art-therapy group: in front of a cherry tree in bloom of women and a child from Mongolia who have presented a dance in public, with long white veils that they made with women from the village. In a room where a series of cuckoo clocks are hung against a fir tree wall, a

fermée, tient, levé dans sa main droite, un masque dont la bouche est ouverte. Comme pour parler.
Plus loin, des réfugiés de Tchétchénie, Géorgie, Afghanistan ont enveloppé dans des couvertures on dirait des silhouettes. Effondrées au pied d'une chaise.
Et sur une sorte de civière, comme une forme humaine enserrée dans des papiers et tissus blancs, ligotée avec des sparadraps. Muselée avec un masque blanc.

Un pays-Heimat. Où déposer vos cris sans mots émotions mémoires traumatismes au-delà de toutes les langues. Un travail. Un chemin. Collectif. Jamais isolé. Toujours en compagnonnage.
Un homme du village au visage grave regarde sur un pan de mur une série de dessins au crayon noir un tunnel jusqu'à un horizon grillagé.
Et votre Heimatmuseum : comme un pays. Un seuil de pays où avoir le droit d'entrer de dire se dire sans paroles se rencontrer ceux d'ici et ceux d'ailleurs partager un repas aux senteurs et saveurs de si loin des liens se sont noués des amitiés beaucoup de ces réfugiés ces demandeurs d'asile ont appris la langue appris un métier habitent le village –

et sont devenus des voisins –

woman from Mongolia, mouth closed, holds, lifts in her right hand, a mask whose mouth is open. As if to speak. Further away, refugees from Chechnya, Georgia, Afghanistan are wrapped up in blankets they look like silhouettes. Collapsed at the foot of a chair. And on a sort of stretcher, a human form wrapped in white paper and fabric tied with band-aids. Muzzled with a white mask.

A Heimat-country. Where to put your cries without words emotions memories traumas beyond all languages. A work. A road. Collective. Never isolated. Always in companionship. A man from the village with a serious face looks at a series of designs in black pencil on a piece of wall a tunnel to a wire-mesh horizon.
And your Heimatmuseum: like a country. A threshold of a country where one has the right to enter to speak to one another to speak without words to meet those from here and elsewhere to share a meal with the scents and flavors of so far away links of friendship are forged many of these refugees these asylum seekers have learned the language learned a trade live in the village—

and have become neighbors—

post-scriptum

Dans le sous-sol du musée aménagé dans le bâtiment de l'ancienne « Gendarmerie » vous avez gardé en l'état ces cellules de prison dans lesquelles furent enfermées des femmes. On voit encore les « messages » grattés sur les parois. En lettres cyrilliques. C'étaient des prisonnières de l'armée nazie, Ukrainiennes soumises aux travaux forcés à Montafon. En 2007, directeur du musée, Andreas Rudigier chercha quelqu'un pour traduire ces graffitis. C'est une réfugiée d'Ukraine qui déchiffra ces pauvres paroles...*je suis là je ne sais pas pourquoi* –

post-script

In the basement of the remodeled museum, the building of the former "Gendarmerie," you have preserved these prison cells in which women were locked up. One still sees the "messages" scratched on the walls. In Cyrillic letters. They were prisoners of the Nazi army. Ukrainians subjected to forced labor at Montafon. In 2007, the director of the museum, Andreas Rudigier searched for someone to translate this graffiti. A female refugee from Ukraine deciphered these sad words ... *I am here I don't know why—*

non-lieu

à Svetlana Alexievitch

Pour elles, j'ai tissé un large drap mortuaire
Avec leurs propres paroles de misère –
Anna Akhmatova

à cette table. La plus petite. Dans le coin le plus inaperçu. Ce matin de juin. Et sa lumière dans le petit jardin de cet hôtel du vieux Paris des écrivains. À voix basse, vous dites combien la poésie vous est vitale et entre toutes celle de Paul Celan –

vos mains elles ont recueilli tant de paroles dans une langue dont les enfants sont les veilleurs comme sur ce dessin une cigogne elle se promène et leurs mots à eux dans une langue qui n'existe pas encore

« Personne n'a rien dit à la cigogne » –

dans un champ noir à Tchernobyl –

no-place

for Svetlana Alexievich

For them, I wove a large shroud
With their own words of misery—
Anna Akhmatova

at this table. The smallest. In the most unnoticeable corner. This June morning. And the light in the small garden of this hotel of the old Paris of writers. In a low voice, you say how much poetry is vital and above all, that of Paul Celan—

your hands have gathered so many words in a language for which children are the guardians of their own words in a language that doesn't exist yet as in this drawing a stork takes a stroll
        "No one said anything to the stork"—

in a black field at Chernobyl—

une voix... comme une maison

ce matin d'avril la mort d'Imre Kertész à Budapest et ta voix cher Aharon Appelfeld ce même matin à Jérusalem :
« *er war ein grosser Freund* »
tous deux votre voix ce parler cet allemand venu de pays de temps de franchissements de frontières et qui n'existe plus métissé de tant de langues d'avoir traversé tant d'exclusions désastres et silences et ce matin d'avril une voix qui t'accueille une intonation qui place l'accent sur la douceur comme une maison grande ouverte –

encore –

a voice... like a house

this April morning the death of Imre Kertész in Budapest and your voice dear Aharon Appelfeld this same morning in Jerusalem:
"*er war ein grosser Freund*"
both of you your voices this way of speaking this German come from countries and times of border crossings that no longer exist cross-bred with so many languages traversed so many exclusions disasters and silences and this April morning a voice that welcomes you an intonation that places the accent on the softness like a house wide open—

still—

habiter la parole

¡ Oh cristalina fuente !

San Juan de la Cruz

comme une lettre à Ignasi Cristià, muséographe scénariste, tandis que nous arpentions ton chantier de la Cartoixa d'Escaladei

le brouillard glacé mettait des larmes dans nos yeux et des fleurs de givre sur la végétation alentour chênes kermès et pins noirs romarins et bruyères et les noisetiers parmi les éclats de roche et les vignobles en terrasse à l'abrupt des montagnes tu avançais dans le silence des ruines retraçant les mémoires des violences de l'Histoire et celles des géographies des lieux et leur ordonnancement au quotidien des vies bibliothèque et réfectoire cour de l'église chapitre et cloître chapelle du sanctuaire et pati dels dolors et comme en contrepoint d'une présence tout aussi irréelle que la blancheur luminescente du brouillard tu traces un paysage intérieur et poses un à un les jalons d'un cheminement vers le cœur du cœur tout au bout du parcours après la dernière cellule reconstituée vestibule et salle de l'Ave Maria cubiculum et oratoire fontaine roseraie et petit bûcher et juste à côté comme en miroir de l'âme rien qu'une boîte noire dans les ruines intactes trace de l'ancienne cellule où chacun isolé près de l'autre habitera dans sa langue –

la parole *el verbo* –

to inhabit the words

> *¡Oh cristalina fuente!*
> San Juan de la Cruz

like a letter to Ignasi Cristià, museographer-scriptwriter, while we surveyed your site of la Cartoixa d'Escaladei

the icy fog put tears in our eyes and flowers of frost on the surrounding vegetation kermes oaks and black pines rosemary heather and hazelnuts among the shards of rock and terraced vineyards at the steep mountains you were climbing in the silence of the ruins retracing memories of the violences of the history and geographies of the places and their daily ordering of lives the library and the refectory church courtyard chapter and cloister of the sanctuary and *pati dels dolors* and in counterpoint to a presence so unreal that in the luminescent whiteness of the fog you trace an interior landscape and place one by one the milestones of a journey toward the heart of the heart at the end of the route after the last reconstituted vestibule cell of the Ave Maria cubiculum and oratory fountain rose garden and small pyre and right next to it as a mirror of the soul nothing but a black box in the untouched ruins trace of the old cell where each one isolated near the other will live in her language—

the words *el verbo*—

petites maisons dans la nuit

petit enfant tu dors profondément dans le pays de ton sommeil je voudrais déposer ces traces de lumière comme autant de petites maisons dans la nuit –

small houses in the night

little child you sleep deeply in the country of your sleep I would like to leave these traces of light like so many small houses in the night—

maison de terre maison de soie

I

les nuits d'été dans ces villages de pisé on entendait les métiers à tisser de l'usine au bout du champ et l'on suivait la voie lactée comme une route de clarté et la vieille voisine avait tiré sa chaise pour la veillée près des jardins et un soir sous les étoiles elle a dit un souvenir d'enfance à douze ans elle travaillait à l'usine et un jour l'inspecteur est passé et on l'avait cachée au milieu des balles de soie pays des pierres glaciaires où il y avait peu de place pour les mots dans le vacarme des métiers et ce soir-là il y a eu le fil de soie de ses paroles comme dévidé d'un cocon secret abri des nuits –

maison de terre maison de soie –

II

filé argent riant sur âme de soie

âme chaîne de soie ils avaient leurs mots d'ouvrage, leurs mots de beauté qui saura le nom du canut qui tissa dans cette échancrure de tulle noir brodé soulevé comme par un souffle tout un champ de fleurs –

house of earth house of silk

I

summer nights in these adobe villages we heard the looms of the factory at the end of the field and we followed the milky way like a bright road and the old neighbor had pulled up her chair near the gardens for the vigil and one evening under the stars she related a childhood memory at twelve years old she was working at the factory and one day the inspector came by and someone had hidden her in the bales of silk the land of glacial stones where there was little room for words in the din of looms and that night there was a silk thread of her words unwinding from a secret cocoon sheltering the nights—

house of earth house of silk—

II

laughing silver thread on a silk core

soul chain of silk they had their words of work, their words of beauty who will know the name of the silk weaver who wove this notch of embroidered black tulle raised as by a puff a whole field of flowers—

III

jonchée de pétales

qui saura jamais le nom du canut qui tissa ce broché *nuances de pétales fraichement tombés de roses jaunes, parfois liserées de lilas ou de carmin ; de roses de couleur incarnadin, liserées de jaune et empourprées de cerise* ; de couleur mauve, magenta foncé ou rouge sang avec des éclats jaunes –

III

littered with petals

who will ever know the name of the silk weaver who wove this brocade *shades of petals freshly fallen from yellow roses, occasionally edged with lilac or carmine; incarnadine colored roses, edged with yellow and blushing cherry red:* purple, dark magenta or blood red with yellow highlights—

IV

tes pauvres mains

Cher ami, que diriez-vous, pour votre moire à
grandes ondes, du nom « l'eau-qui-dort » ?
Colette, 1930 – à Francis Ducharne,
fabricant lyonnais installé à Paris –

un jour, tu l'as sortie de ton armoire, elle était sur un rayon tout en haut, enveloppée pliée dans une toile écrue. Tu l'as posée sur une vieille table de noyer près de la fenêtre qui ouvrait sur ton jardin de légumes et de plantes aromatiques avec une plate-bande de fleurs pour le cimetière zinnias et marguerites glaïeuls et pieds d'alouette et en automne toute en rangées de chrysanthèmes et une à une tu as enlevé les grosses épingles de nourrice qui retenaient les quatre angles de cette toile elle avait cette senteur de linge enfermé de longues années et de lavande fanée et ce fut comme une eau qui dormait depuis tant de décennies presque une vie cette pièce de soie verte et tu l'as ouverte comme une onde réfléchie dans le soleil ton sur ton ces filets bleu moiré et me vient ce mot vietnamien xanh qui dit à la fois le bleu et le vert le ciel miré dans l'émeraude des rizières inondées oui cette pièce d'eau pièce de soie ton chef-d'œuvre à toi tu l'avais tissé dans cette usine-dortoir où tu travaillais les hivers j'imagine ces jours de neige dans l'atelier glacial tes pauvres mains pleines des crevasses des engelures des blessures et usures des travaux de la ferme et par les verrières la clarté plombée de ces ciels noirs dans ces terres froides –

et tes pauvres mains qui tissent ces reflets de lumière –

IV

your poor hands

> *Dear friend, how about the name "sleep-*
> *ing-water" for your cloth of long waves?"*
> Colette, 1930—to Francis Ducharne,
> Lyonnais manufacturer installed in Paris—

one day, you took it out of your armoire, it was on a shelf at the top, folded wrapped in an unbleached linen cloth. You put it on an old walnut table near the window which opened onto your garden of vegetables and aromatic plants with a flower bed for the cemetery zinnias and daisies gladioli and larkspur and in autumn all in rows of chrysanthemums and one by one you removed the large safety pins which held the four corners of this cloth it had the scent of linen locked away for many years and of faded lavender it was like water that had been sleeping for so many decades, almost a lifetime this piece of green silk and you opened it like a wave reflected in the sun tone on tone these blue moiré threads and the Vietnamese word *xanh* comes to me which at the same time conveys the blue and the green the sky mirrored in the emerald of the flooded rice fields yes this piece of water piece of silk your masterpiece you wove it in the factory-dormitory where you worked winters I imagine those snowy days in the freezing workshop your poor hands covered in frostbite crevices of wounds and wear from farm work and through the windows the leaden light and those black skies in these cold lands—

and your poor hands which wove those reflections of light—

ces roseraies du temps des tisseurs de soie

platanes centenaires cèdres du Liban et tulipiers de Virginie le long de l'étang et de ses reflets va cours dans les roseraies mémoires du temps des tisseurs de soie et de ces maîtres dessinateurs-brodeurs qui enseignaient à la classe des fleurs de l'école des Beaux-Arts va cours choisis les roses que tu aimes parfums et couleurs –

tu y apprends que tes chemins de beauté sont d'abord de liberté –

these rose gardens in the days of silk weavers

century-old plane trees cedars from Lebanon and tulip trees from Virginia along the pond and its reflections run through the rose garden memories from the days of the silk weavers and of those master-embroiderers who taught the flower class at the School of Beaux-Arts chose the roses that you love perfumes and colors—

you learn that your paths of beauty started as paths of freedom—

habiter la beauté envers et contre tout

à la mémoire de Suzanne Bukiet

c'est une histoire. Elle a commencé le 25 novembre 1927. Avec une petite fille de onze ans. Myfanwy. Venue à New York. Avec son père. Depuis l'île de Victoria. Au large de Vancouver. Consulter un grand spécialiste. Et ce jour-là elle a su qu'elle ne pourra jamais courir. Sauter. Grimper. Juste et difficilement marcher. Et ce soir-là pour la consoler son père l'a emmenée à Carnergie Hall. Le concerto pour violon de Beethoven. Et sur la scène un petit garçon de onze ans. Yehudi Menuhin. Bien des années plus tard il lui dira : « je suis né cinq jours avant toi pour préparer le monde à ta venue » –
l'histoire de leur amitié nouée quarante-cinq ans plus tard sur cette même île de Victoria, et de la longue suite de portraits que Myfanwy Pavelic fit de Yehudi et son violon saisis sur le vif dans tant de lieux du monde et où par la magie de son pinceau elle donne à entendre ces vibratos ces accents à nuls autres pareils. L'histoire de ce qu'il appelait leur « langue personnelle ». Ce portrait pour la Chambre des Lords, où l'on retrouve ce blason qu'ils élaborèrent ensemble, en exact respect des stricts codes et renfermant cependant les symboles essentiels de Yehudi Menuhin : deux phénix ; cordes et ouïes d'un violon ; deux mains soutenant le globe ; une charrue symbole de la petite ville de Grenchen en Suisse, dont Yehudi fut fait citoyen d'honneur ; le candélabre à sept branches ; en hébreu les mots de tradition hassidique : « *Savoir. Compréhension. Sagesse* » et « *Foi. Espérance. Bonté* ». Et cet étonnant petit tableau qu'il gardait secrètement derrière son bureau. Yehudi lui avait dit un jour en souriant qu'il aimerait apparaître dans un portrait officiel comme un Tzigane partant à la fête assis à contre-sens sur son cheval. C'est cette image qui a inspiré

to inhabit beauty against all odds

in memory of Suzanne Bukiet

it's a story. It began November 25, 1927. With a young girl of eleven, Myfanwy. Came to New York. With her father. From Victoria Island. Off of Vancouver. To consult a great specialist. And that day she found out that she would never be able to run. To jump. To climb. But could only and with difficulty manage to walk. And that night to console her, her father took her to Carnegie Hall. Beethoven's violin concerto. And on stage a young boy of eleven. Yehudi Menuhin. Many years later he would tell her: "I was born five days before you to prepare the world for your coming"—
the story of their friendship formed forty-five years later on this same Victoria Island, and of the long series of portraits Myfanwy Pavelic made of Menuhin and his violin caught on the spot in so many places in the world and where by the magic of her brush she makes these vibratos heard these accents like no other. The story of what he called their "personal language." This portrait for the House of Lords, where we find this blazon they developed together, in exact respect of the strict codes and yet containing the essential symbols of Yehudi Menuhin: two phoenixes; strings and gills of a violin; two hands supporting the globe; a plow symbol of the small city of Grenchen in Switzerland, which made Yehudi an honorary citizen; the seven-branched candelabra; in Hebrew the traditional Hassidic words: "Knowledge. Understanding. Wisdom" and "Faith. Hope. Goodness." And this astonishing small painting that he secretly kept behind his desk. Yehudi told her one day, smiling, that he would love to appear in an official portrait like a Romani going to the celebration sitting sideways on his horse. It's this picture that inspired Myfanwy

à Myfanwy ce tableau-rêve, tableau-Chagall qu'elle lui offrit pour ses quatre-vingts ans. « Il représente, disait-il, tout ce qui est essentiel : la joie et la musique, le monde tzigane, la beauté profonde de l'horizon et la route de la vie toujours ouverte » –
« *We cannot let him go like this* » ce furent mes premiers mots à Myfanwy Pavelic lorsqu'après la mort de Yehudi Menuhin des amis canadiens me procurèrent son numéro de téléphone. La sonnerie retentit dans son atelier tout là-bas sur l'île Victoria. « *Of course, darling, we have to do something, you are welcome anytime.* » Et c'est ainsi que je me suis mise en route. Jusqu'à la péninsule de Saanich. Au nord de Victoria. Dans la vaste maison de Spencer Wood tout en bois et dont les baies ouvraient de tous côtés sur l'Océan. Et son jardin illuminé de fleurs. Ombragé par ces arbres géants multi-centenaires près desquels l'on ressent l'immensité de ces terres. Sapins de Douglas et chênes blancs de l'Oregon thuyas vertigineux et aulnes rouges. Là où Myfanwy avait son atelier et vivait avec son mari et leur fille –
Tessa –
tandis qu'un soir avec son photographe nous choisissions ensemble les portraits qu'elle allait offrir pour *Le Violon de la Paix*, en souriant elle sortit d'un carton une reproduction d'un petit tableau : « *dancing trees* » : « c'était le tableau préféré de Yehudi quand il l'a vu il l'a pris il l'a emporté dans sa chambre et l'a mis dans sa valise. » Un paysage. Une exception dans l'art de Myfanwy peintre de la lumière qui habite les êtres. Petites gens du voisinage à côté de Rostropovitch Glenn Gould Katharine Hepburn Ravi Shankar. Dans son atelier tout un monde de regards. Autant de musiques de l'âme. Comme si par la beauté, Myfanwy réparait chaque fois le désastre de son enfant au visage horriblement déformé par la maladie –

this dream-painting, Chagall-like painting that she gave him for his eightieth birthday. "It represents," he said, "all that is essential: joy and music, the Romani world, the profound beauty of the horizon and the road of life always open"— "*We cannot let him go like this*" those were my first words to Myfanwy Pavelic when after Yehudi Menuhin died his Canadian friends gave me her telephone number. The ringer rang in her studio over there on Victoria Island. "*Of course, darling, we have to do something, you are welcome anytime.*" And that is how I got started. To the Saanich Peninsula. North of Victoria. In the vast house of Spencer Wood all in wood and where the bay windows open on all sides onto the Ocean. And her garden illuminated by flowers. Sheltered by these giant trees each several hundred years old near which one feels the immensity of these lands. Douglas firs and white oaks from Oregon dizzying cedar and red alders where Myfanwy has her studio and lives with her husband and their daughter— Tessa—
while one evening with his photographer together we were choosing portraits that she was going to donate for *Le Violon de la Paix*, with a smile she took out of a cardboard box a reproduction of a small painting: "*dancing trees*": "it was Yehudi's favorite painting when he saw it he took it away to his room and put it in his suitcase." A landscape. An exception to Myfanwy's art, painter of the light which inhabits beings. Ordinary neighborhood people next to Rostropovich Glen Gould Katherine Hepburn Ravi Shankar. In her studio a whole world of faces. So much music of the soul. As if by beauty, Myfanwy was repairing each time the disaster of her child her face horribly deformed by illness—
each painting held a profound human story a rare meeting each time and in her voice soft and reserved a voice that does not intrude she evoked Pierre Trudeau then prime minister of

chacun des tableaux recélait une profonde histoire humaine une rencontre rare chaque fois et de sa voix douce et comme retenue une voix qui ne s'impose pas elle évoqua Pierre Trudeau alors premier ministre et dont elle devait faire le portrait officiel. Il avait fait le voyage jusqu'à Spencer Wood. Une fois le portrait terminé vint le jour de son départ. Il était déjà dans le vestibule son manteau sur le bras son bagage à la main c'était une heure encore très matinale soudain une porte s'ouvre c'est Tessa. Pierre Trudeau lâche son sac de voyage laisse tomber son manteau va au-devant de l'enfant et sans un mot la serre dans ses bras –

whom she was to make the official portrait. He made the trip to Spencer Wood. Once the portrait was finished the day of his departure came. He was already in the hallway his overcoat on his arm his suitcase in hand it was still very early suddenly a door opens it is Tessa. Pierre Trudeau lets go of his travel bag lets his overcoat fall goes up to the child and without a word hugs her tight—

les portes des roulottes arrachées

ce ciel de pleine lune au-dessus des étangs de Camargue. Maria raconte dans la langue manouche qui a les mots de tous les pays traversés. Elle raconte elle était petite fille c'était en Alsace les camions allemands qui sont arrivés sur le campement les hurlements des SS les portes des roulottes arrachées les femmes les enfants poussés à coup de crosses son oncle a couru couper la corde qui attachait leur cheval il allait monter dans le camion quand le soldat allemand a voulu lui arracher son violon alors le vieil homme a levé son violon très haut

et l'a brisé de toutes ses forces –

the doors of the nomads' caravans torn off

the sky of the full moon over the ponds of Camargue. Maria speaks in the Romani language which has the words of all the countries crossed. She says she was a little girl in Alsace when the German trucks arrived at the encampment the howls of the SS the doors of the nomads' caravans torn off the women the children pushed by blows of sticks her uncle ran to cut the rope which held their horse he was going up into the truck when the German soldier tried to tear away his violin then the old man lifted his violin very high

and smashed it with all his strength—

maison de larmes et de lumière

Tan Dun : *Nu Shu, le chant secret des femmes,* symphonie pour harpe, treize microfilms et orchestre.

fil de pluie ruissellement le long des rames rivière des lavandières un monde de sanglots cordes frappées frottées pincées cuivres-soleil et vent-souffle et de chaque bouche les voix en chœur assourdi intense fil d'eau fil de soie sororale pont par-dessus l'abîme lamentos cantilés des entrailles déchirées tracés en broderies mots d'une langue secrète modulés tremblés sur les cordes de la harpe –

maison de larmes et de lumière –

house of tears and light

Tan Dun: *Nu Shu, the secret song of women,* symphony for harp, thirteen microfilms and orchestra.

thread of rain runoff along the oars river of washerwomen a world of sobs strings struck rubbed plucked brass-sun and wind-breath and from each mouth the voices in muffled chorus intense thread of water thread of sisterly silk bridge over the abyss *lamentos cantilés* torn entrails traced in embroidery words of a secret language modulated trembling on the strings of the harp—

house of tears and light—

pierres de lumière

oui commencer par la beauté du monde envers et contre tout ainsi de ce premier matin au seuil d'un long périple à la rencontre des survivants de la famille de Hongrie et leurs descendants au bout de la nuit vous m'avez ouvert votre porte ton regard et tes mains de peintre savent saisir les moindres instantanés dans les embrasures de la vie et aux premières clartés de l'aube tu nous as emmenés voir le lever du soleil sur Jérusalem et chaque pierre était de lumière –

stones of light

yes to start by the beauty of the world against all odds so from this first morning on the threshold of a long journey to meet the survivors of the Hungarian family and their descendants at the end of the night you opened your door to me your look and your skillful painter's hands know to seize the smallest snapshots in the embrasures of life at first light you led us to see the sun rise over Jerusalem and every stone was made of light—

les murs nus de la maison

les salles grises de ce prestigieux lycée parisien et ce matin fatidique l'épreuve d'un concours blanc disserter sur la poésie six heures devant une feuille. Une feuille blanche. Après ce désastre errer dans les rues de Paris et au bord du soir comme un veilleur ce vieux professeur et son offre d'un travail à prendre tout de suite un remplacement dans une école là-bas en Sarre. Partir. La neige fut noire dans les rues sur les toits dans le ciel. Neige noire sur les corons. D'errance en errance trouver un lieu et il y eut ce havre de chaleur cette petite maison de mineurs dans le village de Dudweiler toute de plain-pied la chambre était glaciale mais le cœur de la maison c'était la grande table dans la cuisine le soir autour des épaisses crêpes de pommes de terre. Au milieu de ces montagnes couvertes de forêts que le jeune Goethe découvrit depuis Strasbourg en même temps que les mines d'alun et de houille et qu'il trouva « désertes et tristes » il y eut ce refuge la bibliothèque de l'université sur la porte d'entrée un jour l'annonce d'une soirée avec un poète j'ignorais son nom Pierre Emmanuel je n'avais jamais rencontré de poète j'empruntai le petit volume gris qui venait de paraître chez Seghers il lut et parla et sa voix et ses mots venaient non pas d'un livre mais d'une vie intense d'une quête fervente et chaque mot était comme de prendre un risque et en répondre quand je suis repartie dans la nuit vers la petite maison de mineurs il y avait des mots qui sonnaient plein ce soir-là j'avais découvert l'hospitalité d'un poète de la poésie je veux dire d'une parole donnée et que l'on ne reprend pas et jusqu'à sa mort il y eut l'humanité indéfectible de ce poète sa porte ouverte pour écrire et s'engager quand les poètes de Hanoï furent sous les bombes cette nuit de Noël 1972 sa porte ouverte lorsque je lui rapportai

the bare walls of the house

the gray rooms of this prestigious Parisian high school this fateful morning the test of a mock competition discussing poetry for six hours in front of a sheet. A blank sheet. After this disaster wander the streets of Paris and at the edge of night like a watchman this old professor and his offer to immediately take a job as a substitute teacher in a school over there in Sarre. The snow was black in the streets on the roofs in the sky. Black snow on the miners' cottages. Wandering wandering to find a place and there was this haven of warmth this small house of miners in the village of Dudweiler all on one level the room was glacial but the heart of the house was the large table in the kitchen in the evening around thick potato crêpes. In the middle of these mountains covered with forests that the young Goethe discovered coming from Strasbourg at the same time he discovered the mines of alum and coal which he found "deserted and sad" there was this refuge the university library on the front door one day the announcement of an evening with a poet I did not know his name Pierre Emmanuel I had never met a poet I borrowed a small gray volume just published by Seghers he read and spoke and his voice and words were coming not from a book but from an intense life and fervent quest and every word was like taking a risk and being answerable for them when I left in the night for the small house of miners there were words that sounded full of that evening I discovered the hospitality of a poet of poetry that is of a given word that we do not take back and until his death there was the indefectible humanity of this poet his door open to write and engage when the doors of Hanoi were bombed this Christmas night 1972 his door open when I brought back from the GDR the distress

de RDA la détresse de Peter Huchel immédiatement il appela Heinrich Böll pour chercher ensemble un havre pour ce poète et sa famille et quand en pleine nuit de toute urgence il répondit présent pour redonner une parole de vie à cette jeune philosophe et poète paralysée depuis l'enfance et au bout du désespoir –

*les poètes sont les murs nus de la maison
crépis de cris, de sel, de lèvres, de nuages
fondés sur l'infini des larmes et jetés
à l'infini du ciel errant...*

of Peter Huchel immediately he called Heinrich Böll to seek
together a haven for this poet and his family and when in
the middle of the night he urgently answered the call to give
a word of life to this young philosopher and poet paralyzed
since childhood and at the end of despair—

poets are the bare walls of the house
plaster of screams, of salt, of lips, of clouds
created on the infinity of tears and thrown
to the infinity of the wandering sky...

une porte ouverte

avec qui partager ces voix de veilleurs après l'écrasement du Printemps de Prague à qui apporter toutes ces notes et entretiens et mes premières esquisses de traductions de ces deux poètes que je venais de rencontrer en RDA Reiner Kunze Peter Huchel interdits bannis dans leur propre pays ? Je me souviens d'un après-midi dans la chaude lumière des derniers jours d'automne et ce poète haïtien de passage à Paris. Il me demanda de lui lire mes premières esquisses de traductions de leurs poèmes et il entendit avec gravité ces chemins de résistance et soudain il m'a dit :

— écoute il y a une porte à Paris elle est toujours ouverte c'est celle de Maurice Nadeau vas-y !

26 rue de Condé le secrétariat tenu par Geneviève Serreau et ce petit salon un peu dans la pénombre avec des fauteuils de velours rouge il y avait un romancier et d'être là pour voir Nadeau cela faisait comme un lien tacite on a échangé quelques mots –
Maurice Nadeau est apparu dans l'embrasure il portait un costume de gros velours côtelé son fauteuil était dos à la fenêtre dans son bureau minuscule chaque livre était une présence humaine abritée réfugiée là. Une hospitalité qui accueillait. Sans compter. Et t'offrait un espace d'écriture comme dans une grande maison de la pensée où déposer ta part d'espoir et de combat de solidarité et de beauté quelque chose rapporté de loin dans l'humain menacé –

oui le risque fou de l'hospitalité –

an open door

with whom to share these watchmen's voices after the crushing of the Prague Spring to whom to bring all these notes and interviews and my first translation sketches of these two poets I had just met in GDR Reiner Kunze Peter Huchel forbidden banned in their own countries? I remember an afternoon in the warm light of these last days of autumn when this Haitian poet was passing through Paris. He asked me to read him my first translation sketches of their poems and he heard with gravity these paths of resistance and suddenly he told me:

—listen there is a door in Paris that is always open it is Maurice Nadeau's go there!

26 rue de Condé the secretariat run by Geneviève Serreau and this small living room in the half-light with red velvet armchairs there was a novelist and to be there to see Nadeau seemed an unspoken link we exchanged a few words—
Maurice Nadeau appeared in the doorway he wore a large corduroy suit his armchair was back against the window in his tiny office every book was a sheltered human presence taking refuge there. A hospitality that welcomed. Without counting. And offered you a writing space as in a large house of thought where you can put your share of hope and struggle for solidarity and beauty something brought from afar to the threatened human being—

yes the crazy risk of hospitality—

le mur de la cuisine

et un jour il y eut cette maison je veux dire en ces temps-là on ne comptait pas en mètres carrés mais sur le petit papier dans la vitrine du boulanger c'était écrit deux pièces à elles seules une vraie maison un sourcier aurait tout de suite su qu'il y avait là les sources celles laissées à Mandula utca parmi les étoiles au-dessus du Danube et le vieux cimetière juif des faubourgs de Budapest et cette langue qui se parlait encore rue Elzévir et rue Pavée rue des Rosiers et rue des Écouffes et cette senteur des gâteaux au pavot dans la pâtisserie bleue petite maison de ferveur à la croisée de tant de chemins de traverse et cette évidence de traduire vers tant d'horizons humains havre refuge où pétrir ma langue d'âme avec l'eau de ces sources retrouvées jour et nuit le mur de la cuisine était chauffé par le four du boulanger aux heures des fournées –

dans la cour il y avait une fontaine et aussi dans l'escalier juste avant le palier avec un petit bassin en métal peint –

the kitchen wall

and one day there was this house I mean in those times one didn't count in square meters but on the small paper in the baker's window was written two rooms on their own a real house a dowser would have immediately known there were springs left at Mandula utca among the stars above the Danube and the old Jewish cemetery in the outskirts of Budapest and this language which is still spoken rue Elzévir and rue Pavée rue des Rosiers and rue des Écouffes and this aroma of poppy cakes in the blue bakery little house of fervor at the crossroads of so many side roads and this evidence of translating toward so many human horizons a haven refuge where to knead my soul language with the water of these springs found again day and night the wall of the kitchen was heated by the baker's oven at the hours of the batches—

in the courtyard there was a fountain and also in the staircase just before the landing with a small painted metal basin—

par une nuit de neige

ce fut par une nuit de neige sur Londres une nuit de garde dans les vastes locaux d'Amnesty International déserts en cette Saint-Sylvestre c'est dans cette étrange solitude à la fois perdue dans le grand silence de ces salles et les labyrinthes des couloirs vides et à la fois reliée en alerte au monde par tous les appels qui déchiraient la nuit c'est là, cette nuit-là, que j'ouvris un cahier tout neuf et commençai la traduction du premier vers du premier poème du premier recueil de Nelly Sachs : *Éclipse d'Étoile*

Ô les cheminées
sur les demeures de la mort « ingénieusement » pensées

je n'allai pas plus loin que ces tout premiers mots et déjà, je m'en souviens si bien, je butais sur cet adverbe « *sinnreich* » lesté de toute la perverse performance dont est capable l'intelligence humaine. Je perçus immédiatement que le traduire impliquait de creuser dans les galeries les plus noires de l'humain, de s'engager soi-même dans cette « *traversée de toute poussière par la souffrance et par l'âme* » selon les mots de Nelly Sachs dans une lettre à Paul Celan. Sans doute n'était-ce pas un hasard si j'avais choisi justement ce moment et cet endroit pour ouvrir ce chantier de traduction, une à une soulever les pierres et le poids de plomb de chaque pas, chaque mot dans cette poésie de l'extrême de la souffrance au seuil de ce qui allait devenir un long travail, vivre le compagnonnage de tous ces réseaux de solidarité, en résonance avec ces veilleurs de l'humain, ces gardiens de phare dans les nuits du monde, à la fois dans cette étrange solitude et comme reliée en alerte –

on a snowy night

it was on a snowy night in London a night on call in the vast quarters of Amnesty International deserted on this New Year's Eve it is in this strange solitude at the same time lost in the great silence of these rooms and the labyrinths of empty corridors and at the same time linked in alert to the world by all the calls that were tearing the night apart it is there, that night, that I opened a brand new notebook and began the translation of the first line of the first poem of the first collection by Nelly Sachs: *Star Eclipse*

O the chimneys
on the dwellings of death "ingeniously" thought out

I didn't go further than these very first words and already, I remember it so well, I stumbled on this adverb *"sinnreïch"* weighted by all the perverse performance of which human intelligence is capable. I immediately perceived that translating involved digging into the darkest tunnels of the human being, engaging oneself in this *"passing through all dust by suffering and by the soul"* according to the words of Nelly Sachs in a letter to Paul Celan. No doubt it wasn't chance that I had chosen precisely this moment and this place to open this translation work site, one by one to lift the stones and the lead weight of each step, each word in this poetry of the extremity of suffering at the threshhold of what was going to become a long work, to live the companionship of all these solidarity networks, in resonance with these human watchmen, these lighthouse keepers in the nights of the world, at the same time in this strange solitude and as if connected on alert—

dans l'urgence et dans l'infinie durée –

urgently and indefinitely—

la lumière des mots

comme une lettre à Jean Halpérin

au bout de vos exils il y eut votre pièce lumineuse vos livres et près de votre bureau la ferveur et la pénombre de ces visages sur une photo de Frédéric Brenner ces visages si intenses. D'avant. Avant la Shoah. Et votre table d'hospitalité pour les repas du shabbat et les veillées des grandes Fêtes –

votre maison de lumière je veux dire la lumière des mots –

cette lumière que vous m'avez appris à extraire des pierres de nuit dans le chant de Nelly Sachs –

the light of words

like a letter to Jean Halpérin

at the end of your exiles there was your radiant room your books and near your desk the fervor and penumbra of these faces in a photo by Frédéric Brenner these faces so intense. Before. Before the Shoah. And your hospitality table for the Sabbath meals and the eves of the major holidays—

your house of light I mean the light of words—

this light that you taught me to extract from the stones of night in the song of Nelly Sachs—

le Paradou

c'est à un jeune couple iranien en résidence au collège international des traducteurs que je dois d'avoir pris cette petite route qui longe les premiers amandiers en fleurs au cœur de l'hiver et les montagnes bleues des Alpilles. Jusqu'au village du Paradou avec ses lavoirs profonds et dont le nom sait le labeur du moulin à foulon. Jusqu'à cette maison cachée au creux d'une petite place et dès que tintait la clochette résonnait la voix chaleureuse au subtil accent hongrois de Ladislas Mandel qui montait lentement les marches jusqu'à la petite grille et t'ouvrait un jardin de fleurs et d'arbres fruitiers de petites allées et d'ombrages et dans la longue pièce en soupente te conduisait au cœur des écritures du monde et leurs alphabets leurs outils et leurs supports coques de fruits et terres cuites parchemins cailloux et coquillages talismans et tatouages amulettes et moulins à prières... oui, tenir dans tes mains tous ces objets témoins et vous écouter raconter leur histoire. Dans la lumière tamisée de la petite fenêtre taillée dans les épais murs de pierre vous m'avez donné de découvrir que l'écriture est un langage et que la graphie donne à voir jusqu'à l'indicible –

et au bord du soir en reprenant la petite route j'emportais comme un talisman cette dernière phrase sur le seuil : *n'oublie pas : la calligraphie trouve ses sources d'inspiration à l'intérieur de chacun de nous* –

passionnée de calligraphie depuis longtemps je recherchais les meilleures plumes, les encres les plus noires, mais ma main restait muette, je butais sur les lettres, je ne savais pas qu'elles étaient en moi, immémoriales : les lettres de l'alphabet

le Paradou

it is thanks to a young Iranian couple in residence at the International College of Translators that I must have taken this little road that runs along the first blooming almond trees in the heart of winter and the blue mountains of the Alpilles. Up to the village of Paradou with its deep wash houses and its fulling mill whose name knows its labor. Up to this house hidden in the hollow of a small square and as soon as the bell rang the warm voice of Ladislas Mandel with his subtle Hungarian accent resonating as he slowly climbed the steps to the small gate and let you in to a garden of flowers and fruit trees small alleyways and shade and in the long attic room led you to the heart of writings of the world and their alphabets their tools and their supports fruit shells and terracotta parchments pebbles and shells talismans tattoos amulets and prayer wheels... yes, to hold in your hands all these witnesses and to listen to you recount their history. In the filtered light of the small window carved into the thick stone walls you had me discover that writing is a language and that spelling reveals the unspeakable—

and at the edge of evening taking the little road again I carried this last sentence on the threshold like a talisman: *don't forget: calligraphy finds its sources of inspiration within each of us—*

passionate about calligraphy for a long time I looked for the best quills, the blackest inks, but my hand remained silent, I butt against the letters, I didn't know they were within me, immemorial: the letters of the Hebrew alphabet. And starting like a small child to calligraph them, learning the gesture,

hébraïque. Et en commençant comme un petit enfant à les calligraphier, en apprenant le geste, le souffle de chacune d'elles ce fut soudain comme des retrouvailles, comme si j'entendais la voix de ferveur de mon grand-père Nathan –

the breath of each of them was suddenly like a reunion, as if I could hear the fervent voice of my grandfather Nathan—

langue d'âme

petite maison que tu emportes comme un violon là où il y a
le chant des sources –

là où habiter et près de la croisée au petit matin calligraphier
la lumière des mots –

speech of the soul

little house that you carry like a violin where lies the song of springs—

where to live near the crossroads in early morning to calligraph the light of words—

pour Y.

c'était dans ces terres si froides terres des brouillards transis qui les jours d'été montent des combes sombres au fond du vallon et constellent de fleurs les matins d'hiver ton premier hiver traçant la neige nous sommes partis comme pour un grand voyage à la rencontre du soleil au-dessus des nuages écouter le chant des sources le long des talus où l'eau file comme un serpent de lumière sous la glace –

for Y.

it was in these lands such cold lands of numb fogs which on summer days rise from the dark nooks at the bottom of the valley and spangle winter mornings with flowers your first winter tracing snow we left as if for a great voyage to meet the sun above the clouds to listen to the song of springs along the banks where water rushes like a snake of light under the ice—

une maison à tous les horizons

pour Marc Riboud

en ces derniers jours d'été vous nous avez quittés et soudain comme sorti d'une chambre noire dans le souvenir votre retour de Hué « Une ville assassinée » ainsi que vous l'écriviez neuf jours après l'assassinat de Martin Luther King. Et au bout de toutes ces terres de l'extrême il y avait ce havre rue Christine ces locaux des années pionnières de l'Agence Magnum en bas près de la porte d'entrée la petite cafétéria enfumée bruissant comme une ruche où jour et nuit arrivaient les photographes reporters du monde entier et au sommet de l'étroit escalier sur les tables tous les clichés planches contact coupures de presse boîtes d'archives et cette odeur des tirages frais sortis des labos –

une maison à tous les horizons –

a house for all horizons

for Marc Riboud

in these last days of summer you left us and suddenly as if coming out of a darkroom in the memory of your return from Hué "an assassinated city" as you wrote nine days after the assassination of Martin Luther King. And at the end of all these extreme lands there was this haven rue Christine these premises from the pioneer days of the Magnum Agency downstairs near the front door of the small smoky cafeteria rustling like a beehive where day and night photographers reporters from all over the world arrived and at the top of the narrow staircase on the tables all the pictures contact sheets press clippings archival boxes and this odor of fresh prints from the labs—

a house for all horizons—

une maison où revenir envers et contre tout

partir d'un petit port de pêche ou de quelque embarcadère au fond d'une crique au gré des marées et des courants accoster sur des pontons de fortune l'eau du seul puits de l'île la lumière des lampes de poche ou des bougies tout autour de toi les murmures et chuchotements les voix et les appels les claquements des becs et les frottements des ailes ces grands voyageurs venus de tous les continents sur ces rochers et falaises battus par les vents jour et nuit sans bruit à pas de silence tu te fais oiseau parmi les oiseaux et eux se font habitants de la terre le temps juste le temps de donner vie et préparer leurs petits pour la migration prochaine –

a house to come back to against all odds

to leave from a small fishing port or from some pier at the bottom of a cove at the tides and currents to dock on makeshift pontoons water from the only well on the island light from flashlights or candles all around you murmurs and whispers voices and calls the slapping of beaks and the rubbing of wings of these great travelers come from every continent on the rocks and cliffs beaten by the winds day and night without a sound with silent steps you become a bird among the birds and they become inhabitants of the earth the time just the time to give life and to prepare their young for the coming migration—

Skokholm Island
mi-juin

falaises de grès rose noircies par les algues effilées par les vents en lames dressées le long des précipices éclat blanc des silènes maritimes aux effluves de miel et parmi les rochers et bris de pierre mourons écarlates et petites étoiles des oreilles de souris cœur jaune des matricaires et flammes vives des renoncules ils sont de retour sur leur île nue pour seule ombre celle des ailes –

et soudain dans cette solitude de pierre des bouquets de tout petits myosotis et au revers d'une motte de terre des pensées sauvages bleu de nuit avec un liseré de lumière –

il y a comme des petites clairières de jacinthes des bois traces des forêts disparues –

tourbe et rocs en affleurement tout un monde souterrain galeries et terriers des oiseaux de mer terre aride où ils reviennent des continents et océans retrouver leurs petites maisons creusées profond sous les herbes des vents tout un monde de survie que tu ignores quand tu marches dessus quittant l'étroit sentier balisé terre fragile leur terre natale où donner la vie –

Skokholm Island
mid-June

cliffs of pink sandstone blackened by seaweed sharpened by the winds in blades erect along the precipices white burst among the honey fragrance of maritime silenes and among the rocks and broken stones scarlet pimpernels and little stars mouse ears yellow heart of matricaria and lively flames of buttercups they are back on their naked island only wings for shadow—

and suddenly in this stone solitude bouquets of tiny forget-me-nots and on the back of a clod of earth wild thoughts of night blue with a border of light—

there are small glades of bluebells of wood traces of forests disappeared—

an outcrop of peat and rocks a whole underground world galleries and burrows of seabirds arid land where they return from continents and oceans to find their little homes buried deep under the wind-blown grass an entire world of survival that you ignore when you step on it leaving the narrow-marked path fragile earth their native land where they give life—

macareux moine

I

revenus de si loin leur temps devient le tien ils vaquent à deux pas de toi si étrangers si familiers sortent de leur terrier avec un peu de terre autour du bec déambulent épient scrutent soudain courent prendre l'élan piquer vers la mer tout en bas disparaître profond dans l'eau remonter le bec plein de poissons filer sous terre vers le petit tout au fond –

II

brusque vent de panique les grandes ailes des goélands jettent leur ombre sur les terriers les macareux s'enfoncent sous la terre montent la garde courent en rangs serrés vers le promontoire s'envolent sans un cri –

III

debout au bord de la falaise face aux vents déchaînés ils sont leur propre petite maison –

IV

sur la pente herbeuse ils sont là debout à l'entrée de leurs terriers comme autant de petites cabanes de transhumants sur un alpage dans cette lumière du soir –

puffins

I

returned from so far away their time becomes yours they are walking a stone's throw from you so strange so familiar they come out of their burrow with a little bit of dirt around their beak they wander around watch scrutinize suddenly run to gather momentum to dive towards the sea to the very bottom to disappear deep in the water to resurface with a beak full of fish to dash off underground towards the little one at the very bottom—

II

sudden wind of panic the great wings of the gulls cast their shadow on the burrows the puffins sink into the earth stand guard run in tight rows toward the promontory fly away without a cry—

III

standing at the edge of the cliff in the face of raging winds they are their own little home—

IV

on the grassy slope they are there standing at the entrance of their burrows like so many small transhumant huts on an alpine pasture in this evening light—

pétrel tempête

nichés au fond des cavités dans les falaises au-dessous du phare tu ne les verras pas de tout le jour c'est la nuit qu'ils sortent pêcher fondus dans l'obscurité pour éviter les attaques des mouettes dans le long crépuscule de ce solstice d'été sous un ciel de cristal bleu nuit la lune jetait un pont d'or sur la mer soudain un vol de fines ailes noires a piqué tournoyé à contre-clarté fulgurant comme en alerte et puis est reparti tout aussi soudain dans les roches escarpées c'est tout ce que j'aurai vu de cet oiseau dont on dit qu'il est le plus petit des migrateurs et revient de Mauritanie et d'Afrique du Sud et on raconte aussi que lorsque les marins les voyaient se poser sur le bateau c'était signe de gros temps qui menaçait –

storm petrel

nestled at the bottom of cavities in cliffs above the lighthouse you will not see them all day long it is at night that they go out to fish melting in the dark to avoid seagull attacks in the long twilight of this summer solstice under a crystal blue night sky the moon was throwing a bridge of gold on the sea suddenly a flight of thin black wings darted twirled backlit swift as though on alert and then set off again just as suddenly in the steep rocks this is all I will have seen of this bird which is said to be the smallest of the migrators returned from Mauritania and South Africa and it is also said that when the sailors saw them land on the boat it was a sign of bad weather menacing—

puffin des Anglais

au petit matin le long des falaises parmi les fleurs et les bris de pierres les corps dépecés de puffins des Anglais eux aussi sortent la nuit pour aller pêcher l'un des deux garde le terrier –

English puffins

in the early morning along the cliffs among the flowers and broken stones the fleshless bodies of English puffins also come out at night to go fishing one of the two guards the burrow—

comme un message à N.D.
qui travaille sur l'île avec l'observatoire
du Wildlife du Pays de Galles

I

cette nuit-là tu avais enregistré le dialogue de quarante minutes entre le mâle et la femelle d'un couple de puffins des Anglais au fond de leur terrier –

II

> *avant la musique, pour moi, il y avait les sons, avant que le son devienne musique le son était un vecteur, le son, le bruit, la mélodie, le timbre, était un vecteur presque plus fort que les mots*
> Sonia Wieder-Atherton

tu rêves de pouvoir un jour reconnaître entre mille chacun de ces oiseaux migrateurs quand il reviendra la saison prochaine entre mille reconnaître ses sons ses bruits ses mouvements ses cris. Son langage –

et à la place d'une bague connaître à sa voix le pétrel tempête-

like a message to N.D.
who works on the island with the observatory
of Wildlife of the Country of Wales

       I

that night you recorded the forty-minute dialogue between the male and female couple of English puffins at the bottom of their burrow—

       II

> *before music, for me, there were sounds, before sound became music sound was a vector, sound, noise, melody, timbre, was a vector almost louder than words*
> **Sonia Wieder-Atherton**

you dream of one day being able to recognize among a thousand each one of these migratory birds when it will return next season among a thousand to recognize its sounds its noises its movements its cries. Its language—

and instead of a band know by its voice the storm petrel—

Farne Islands
début août

dans le petit port de Seahouses en levant l'ancre ce matin les pêcheurs ont bien dit : « Ils sont partis. Hier, il ne restait que deux sternes arctiques » –

au bord du ciel de pluie il y a des cumulus lumineux avec des lacs de cratères bleu translucide le bateau longe les falaises et leur silence déjà d'absence et en une danse d'adieu tout autour du fanal où par temps de brouillard on allumait des feux d'alarme deux paires d'ailes si blanches si fines à peine le poids d'une grande lettre tournoient avant l'envol plus au nord où se fortifier puis jusqu'à l'Antarctique où elles arriveront en novembre et sur l'île déserte les terriers des oiseaux sont vides sous le vent tremblent les étendues de ciguë vert pâle et les chardons gris perle et au milieu des herbes déjà noires un macareux tout seul parmi de minuscules myosotis et les reflets argentés des derniers silènes maritimes quelques petits s'entraînent sur les vagues le ciel de plomb est si bas que l'eau a des couleurs de nuit mais soudain une éclaircie trace un pont d'argent et puis sur la tourbe humide il y a cette senteur des hautes menthes drues récemment arrachées pour quand les sternes arctiques vont revenir faire leurs nids –

Farne Islands
early August

in the small port of Seahouses upon raising anchor this morning the fishermen said firmly: "They are gone. Yesterday, there were only two Arctic terns left"—

at the edge of the rainy sky there are bright cumulus clouds with translucent blue crater lakes the boat runs alongside the cliffs and their silence already of absence and in a farewell dance all around the lantern where in foggy weather we lit alarm fires two pair of wings so white so thin barely the weight of a large letter they twirl before flight further north where they fortify themselves until Antarctica where they will arrive in November and on the desert island the bird burrows are empty the expanses of pale green hemlock and pearl gray thistles tremble in the wind and among the already black grass a puffin all alone among the miniscule forget-me-nots and the silvery reflections of the last maritime silenes a few little ones practice on the waves the leaden sky is so low that the water has colors of night but suddenly a sunny spell traces a silver bridge and then on the damp peat there is the scent of tall mint recently pulled up for when the Arctic terns will come back to make their nests—

pétales et parfum Rose de Damas

il est posé sur la table de la cuisine où j'écris ce soir du 16 XII 16. Posé comme un petit talisman de cinq centimètres de côté. Un savon d'Alep. Et sur le papier de soie mauve un peu rêche qui l'enveloppe une étiquette vert pâle : « *fait main oliviers sauvages huile d'amande douce pétales et parfum Rose de Damas entièrement artisanale et manuelle* ». Et le nom du village. Et le nom du savonnier – Alep. Ils ont froid. Ils ont faim. Quarante mille sur deux kilomètres carrés. Évacuer. « *Vider.* » Un mot qui, depuis « les temps modernes », « *s'emploie généralement en parlant d'un groupe que l'on renvoie "en masse"* » *(Le Grand Robert)* – renvoyer ? mais où ?

et ce soir, dans le journal, cette photo d'Alep un vieil homme penché à la fenêtre d'un convoi de bus son visage sanglote comme de n'avoir plus de larmes les yeux baissés sur une main d'adieu tendue vers la sienne mais déjà les mains ne s'atteignent plus arrachées l'une de l'autre en partance. Et les sources sous les bombes les armes chimiques les ruines les sources si elles avaient tari avec les larmes du vieil homme ? –

Damask Rose petals and perfume

it is placed on the kitchen table where I am writing this evening of December 16, 2016. Placed like a small talisman five centimeters across. Aleppo soap. And on the slightly rough mauve tissue paper wrapped around it a pale green label: "*handmade wild olive vines sweet almond oil Damask Rose petals and perfume entirely artisanal and manual.*" And the name of the village. And the name of the soap maker— Aleppo. They are cold. They are hungry. Forty thousand on two square kilometers. To evacuate. "*To empty.*" A word which, since "modern times," "*is generally used in speaking of a group that one sends away "en masse.*" (*Le Grand Robert*)— to send away? but where?

and this evening, in the newspaper, this photo of Aleppo an old man leaning out of a convoy bus window his face sobs as though having run out of tears his eyes lowered on a farewell hand extended toward his but already hands no longer reach torn apart in parting. And the springs under the bombs the chemical weapons the ruins the springs as if they dried up with the old man's tears?—

nuit

« *les gens aiment le mot refuge,
ils n'aiment pas les réfugiés* »
Élie Wiesel

comme une lettre
pour ceux qui m'ont accueillie au Grand-Saint-Bernard

ombres et lumières sur la voûte de la crypte creusée profond dans la roche depuis plus de mille ans les petites flammes tracent comme des étoiles oui prendre la route jusqu'ici. Pour une question. Juste une question : en ce lieu extrême à quelques pas de la frontière y-a-t-il encore une porte ouverte par tous les temps à tous les venants ?

passé le porche tout de suite dans l'entrée à droite tu trouveras un petit portillon avec écrit dessus *nuit* pour appeler un chanoine à n'importe quelle heure par n'importe quelle tempête je l'ai attendu dans le couloir devant la cuisine où il était de service et quand il est sorti autour d'une petite table je lui ai posé ma question. Pour laquelle j'avais pris la route –

— *Oui, la porte est ouverte. Sans rien demander. Six réfugiés viennent d'arriver. Certains de Syrie. Avec quelqu'un de la maison ils apprennent à bâtir en pierres sèches* –

le brouillard qui s'est levé le matin avait un goût de source –

night

> *people like the word refuge,*
> *but they don't like the refugees*
> **Elie Wiesel**

like a letter
for those who welcomed me at the Grand-Saint-Bernard

shadows and lights on the vault of the crypt dug deep in the rock for more than a thousand years the little flames twinkle like stars yes take the road here. For one question. Just one question: in this extreme place a few steps from the border is there still a door open in all weather for all comers?

immediately past the porch in the entry on the right you will find a small gate with *night* written above it to call a clergy-man at any time through any storm I waited for him in the hallway in front of the kitchen where he was on duty and when he came out around a small table I asked him my question. The one for which I took the road—

> —Yes, the door is open. No questions asked. Six refugees just arrived. Some from Syria. With someone from the house they learn to build with dry stones—

the fog that rose in the morning tasted like a spring—

le point de rencontre

le point de rencontre ce fut à la sortie du métro sur cette petite place déserte en ce matin de gris et de froid le temps juste le temps assis tous ensemble dans l'unique pièce avec tous les livres et le monocorde accroché au mur et les fleurs sur la vieille table de noyer près de la fenêtre oui nos hôtes du Darfour Hamad y étudia les littératures d'Afrique mais aussi Victor Hugo et Kundera traduits en arabe et il apprend le français et sur son coin de table au Foyer il a déjà deux livres et il emportera comme un talisman les *Contemplations* et le dictionnaire des enfants ne pas poser de questions laisser les paroles à leur source le temps juste le temps de parler ici la langue de votre pays et retrouver les saveurs des plats familiers et le bien-être est monté comme une évidence de confiance et ce jour-là j'ai compris que l'hospitalité c'est devenir à notre tour vos hôtes et soudain dans le grand soleil de midi il y a eu cet espace pour dire avec vos mots à vous vos routes d'exil vos mots comme une maison partagée –

the meeting point

the meeting point was at the metro exit on this deserted small square this gray and cold morning time only time seated all together in this single room with all the books and the monochord hooked on the wall and the flowers on the old walnut table near the window yes our hosts from Darfur Hamad studied African literature there but also Victor Hugo and Kundera translated into Arabic and he is learning French and on his corner of the table in the Foyer he already has two books and he will carry like a talisman *The Contemplations* and a children's dictionary don't ask questions leave the words to their origin time only time to speak here the language of your country and rediscover the flavors of familiar dishes and well-being rose as evidence of confidence and that day I understood that hospitality is to become at our turn your hosts and suddenly in the full noon sun there was this space to say with your own words your roads of exile your words like a shared house—

post-scriptum

*notes d'un voyage à Bâle
exposition Chagall XII 17*

I

comme une lettre à Max et Christiane Milner –

ce petit matin de décembre le train longe les vignobles et les coteaux au loin et soudain ce fut comme un pèlerinage dans ce jour qui n'est pas encore levé la maison de Fixin tout en haut du chemin au milieu des vignes autour de la longue table dans la cuisine l'intensité des joies et des ferveurs des larmes et des pensées puis la nuit dans les épais murs de pierre les petites fenêtres aux vitres étoilées de givre et de rêves tout au fond de la brume bleue il y a un feu au bord de l'hiver l'âme d'une maison habite un paysage longtemps après tous les départs et sans bruit métamorphose ses neiges et ses soleils au cadran des souvenirs –

II

1913
et dans la neige sur les toits un violon bleu et cette bougie dans un candélabre et toute la douceur des yeux d'un animal du monde des bergers et dans les airs cette carriole emportée et au bord du vide embrasé une petite maison couleur d'incendie –

post-script

notes on a trip to Basel
Chagall exhibition December 17

I

like a letter to Max and Christiane Milner—

this early December morning the train goes along the vineyards and distant hills and suddenly it was like a pilgrimage on this day that hasn't yet begun the house of Fixin at the very top of the path between the vines around the long table in the kitchen the intensity of joys and passions of tears and thoughts then the night in the thick stone walls the small windows with starry panes of frost and of dreams deep in the blue mist there is a fire on the edge of winter the soul of a house inhabits a landscape long after all departures and silently transforms its snows and suns to the dial of memories—

II

1913
and in the snow on the roofs a blue violin and this candle in a candelabra and all the softness of the eyes of an animal from the shepherds' world and in the air this cart carried away and at the edge of the void a small house blazes the color of fire—

1914
et dans la neige des rues une carriole emporte un pauvre
déménagement une bêche une chaise un balluchon –
dans la neige des rues une carriole emporte un cercueil –

« gouache sur papier sur carton » mon père et la grand-mère
entre ces deux visages crépusculaires un chat au reflet blanc
dans ce monde couleur de cendre et de nuit dans des légendes on dit qu'il a des braises dans les yeux et veille sur l'âtre
génie protecteur du foyer –

« encre de chine, blanc sur papier» les réfugiés
un homme marche penché sur un chat tracé en blanc il l'emporte dans sa main comme un trésor. Comme sur une route
d'exode –

III

c'était le soir le chef de gare s'est approché : « ne restez pas
dehors !» un vent glacial soufflait sur le quai et dans le hall
de passage soudain tous ces inconnus les mains tendues vers
une colonne chauffante à infra-rouges tous en rond comme
autour d'un foyer le temps juste le temps entre deux trains
de devenir un peu humains –

1914
and in the snowy streets a cart carries away a poor removal
a spade a chair a bundle—
in the snowy streets a cart carries away a coffin—

"gouache on paper on cardboard" my father and grandmother between these two crepuscular faces a cat with a white reflection in this ash-colored night-colored world in legends it is said he has embers in his eyes and watches over the hearth the protective genie of the home—

"India ink, white on paper" the refugees a man walks leaning over a cat traced in white, he carries it in his hand like a treasure. Like on a road of exodus—

III

it was in the evening the station master approached: "don't stay outside!" an icy wind was blowing on the platform and in the passage hall suddenly all these strangers' hands extended toward an infra-red heating column all in a circle as if around a hearth the time just the time between two trains to become a little human—

Afterword

IN THE BEGINNING OF Mireille Gansel's *Soul House*, we hear the question of a little boy, springing from a waiting heart, simple, obvious and serious. It is born of the moment of a springtime word, lively and refreshing. It irrigates the entire collection. A slight anxiety emerges, too, as from a dream: what to do with the distance of time, distance and origins? Could this anxiety delay the response to the child's question, give reason to his emotion, and soothe him? He is to be the custodian of a story of tireless departures towards distant roads and their intersections. He'll be given "the hand of words" with which to approach the rich silt of a life and let his imagination wander the traces which may become familiar to him.

yes you're right it was pretty my house when I was little

Returning to the child's words, we know that he is the common thread, the first of a weft on which to weave a large canvas for a "geography of the heart," which Gansel, translator and poet, calls "the force of attraction." To requests that were most often friendly, often urgent and granted to her inner demands, she responded by "taking to the road," even if it meant going farther afield—as if to experience the traces that would remind her of the very paths of returning to the "native country."

In the morning brightness of that first day, the singing charm and the fervor of the child were the prelude to an efflorescence of memory images, and with them a rich harvest of words from elsewhere and everywhere. Thus was made, spontaneously, the outline of a pact or a commitment concluded, hand in hand, for narratives, stories, sometimes

barely suggested, with the words and writings of many languages, or even "beyond all languages."

What generosity, in the recovery of the encounters experienced over the years, so often accompanied by the lights of certain April mornings: black lights of distress or lights of new beginnings. The awakened memories, of exiled lives, of survivals, of unspeakable pain. And the warm memories of voices, thresholds, and tables of dialogue and hospitality. Having brought them to the surface also meant assuming the risk and the responsibility of answering for them.

It had to be said how the discoveries of others, neighborhoods, were made in a large number of places and villages in the world. Adobe houses, caravans, tents in the sand, houses overlooking the river, houses all open to the ocean, and cliff burrows. Like sanctuaries of security, and more secret cocoons: we all know the game of hide and seek, nestled in the caress of fabrics! Here, there are bales of silk where to hide the daughter of a weaver worker, too young a worker in the family trade. There's also the accomplishment of so many collective works, paintings by several hands, choreographed dances and music and choirs. Creations initiated and collected on the paths of exile, of refuge, and of life: these paths that make the world "habitable."

In *Le Violon de la Paix*—a book of several artists' voices and hands, and for which Mireille Gansel was accompanist and translator—Yehudi Menuhin draws on the journeys and dreams of a child-violinist to express his need and his passion to "feel under his feet the solid ground of the past," with the music as a "password" to everywhere in the world. With an irrepressible surge of courage and freedom Menuhin transmits the keys and traditions of his commitments, with respect for all peoples, the people of the Roma first—"companion in persecution" with the Jews. Thus, he forges links, footbridges,

bridges, however fragile they may be, open to horizons of beauty and peace.

Evoking Menuhin here, in regard to *Soul House*, is to underscore how many and precious are the childish presences in Gansel's book, their complicity and their vocation, how lively their light dancing and musical grace, to climb or descend the slopes of the cities, toward the rivers and their confluences—the Rhône and the Saône of Lyon, the Danube River.... Like a farandole when the children marvel at their steps and their games. Or like, in this close circle, where their faces radiate to discover the very small puppets of the young showman barely guessed in front of the black shreds of the salesman, in the drawing by Francisco Goya. Children who are enchanted by the fabulous trophies of the fairground such as the "fish with golden scales," this same magical fish of so many memories and legends of distant lands and waters.

Children, yes: how did they learn the strength and fidelity of dreams and tenderness, the right to free and joyful imagination, the awakening to beauty, often nestled very far and very deep, and of which they do not know that it can be betrayed, profaned, engulfed in times of irreparable destruction, abysses and darkness? Time of violence without forgiveness.

Let's go back for a moment to this story of Menuhin that Gansel tells in the heart of *Soul House*, anxious to restore its unfolding. An eleven-year-old girl, Myfanwy, whose body was crippled by illness, came with her father to Carnegie Hall to listen to Yehudi—also eleven years old, already a virtuoso musician—perform Beethoven's Violin Concerto. Many years later, Myfanwy Pavelic, a painter, and Menuhin shared a "common language of friendship," of creation. Myfanwy had painted a number of portraits of Yehudi, listening to the trills and vibratos of his violin, as if sounding from his deepest being. So many commitments to the end of

his "always open road of life," to this very desire to be shown "like a Gypsy going to the celebration sitting sideways on his horse." In *Le Violon de la Paix*, this image of the musician entering with his back turned to the future, seems to make an ironic and fraternal sign to Walter Benjamin's Angel of History. But here are all the blues and colors of a ride towards the immensity of a horizon of life, ending in March 1999, in Berlin.

Told in *Soul House*, this story cannot end there. It is, in all Gansel's writing, the matrix of another story, brief and foundational in turn. Myfanwy had just completed the official portrait of Pierre Elliot Trudeau, then Prime Minister, during the 1980s. A new morning, in the distant home on Victoria Island, open entirely to the ocean and immense lands of trees and flowers. Trudeau, guest of the artist, is on the doorstep, ready to leave. "It was still very early morning—suddenly a door opens, it's Tessa."

A young girl, up early, silent. The uncertain features of her face. She is there, all reserve and respect for the visitor—her guest, too—who then puts down his cape magnified in the beautiful colors of the painting and hugs the young girl. It is a moment of tenderness and gratitude, like a pact of Justice and Beauty that reminds us of certain words of Aimé Césaire, in *Moi, laminaire…*

How not to see again these glances at the threshold of their childhood, of girls and boys eleven years old? The Roma children violently torn from the doors of their caravans by the Germans, in front of them a freed horse escapes, an old parent crushes his violin… so many terrifying visions and yet the dignity of gestures and images. I am thinking of the canvases painted by Ceija Stojka, a great Roma artist. Returning to life, surviving Auschwitz, and Ravensbrück, and Bergen Belsen, she will tell in her works the nomadic and happy life of her childhood, soon banned from school, and the distress

in all the eyes of the children and their mothers, hunted down, rounded up, deported with the Jews to the camps and ghettos, then to the extermination camps.

Like Mireille Gansel, we knew and loved the hospitality of the Roma, in their camps and villages, and found with our schoolchildren their own schoolchildren of the same age.

So, the gaze of the young Roma boy at the flower market in Paris. And this moment of Balkan music on the footbridge of Île Saint-Louis...

It is to the mixing and sharing of the waters of the Seine, at the end of the Quai aux Fleurs, under the high windows where the great tutelary figures would pass—philosophers and resistance fighters at the same time, writers, poets, men and women of courage and responsibility, free and faithful to their common commitments... They were the Dreyfusards of the time of Bernard Lazare, they were thinkers of tradition and re-founders of a modernity of Colloquia, the continuing friendship of Judeo-Christians, with a magistracy of rigor and will.

Faithfully, the poems and stories of *Soul House* remind us of familiar names—among them the names of some of our mentors too: Vladimir Jankélévitch, Edmond Fleg, Jean Cassou, Jean Halpérin, Aaron Appelfeld... the poets and their fraternal and united vigils, whether they be poets from Hanoi or the GDR, poets from France and in France—René Char, Pierre Emmanuel, and the other "lighthouse keepers in the nights of the world." It is up to each of us, readers, to renew their encounters, their companionship, to hear their voices uniquely, coming from the languages of their countries: "their words at their source."

So close to all these outstretched hands, in a gesture similar to the weight and richness of the words, the respectful care of the hands, and the rigor of the gaze of Eugénie Goldstern.

Mireille Gansel, from Grenoble, in the libraries of Geneva, London, and Vienna—with ethnologists, anthropologists, architects, and eminent museologists—had herself brought together, translated, and published the forgotten and major texts of this young Jewish ethnologist, born in Odessa in 1884, who, during the first quarter of the twentieth century, shared the lives of the mountaineers of the great Alpine arc, first in Bessans, on the borders of French Savoy, beyond the borders, the valleys and the mountain pastures of the Balkans... How it moves us, this re-discovery of the old shelter houses, and—in their "secret heart"—of all these found toys, primordial, humble, "carved from twigs, bones, shells of fruit, repository of children's dreams and fears." How not to feel nostalgia and pain at the tragic fate of the young woman, Eugénie Goldstern, murdered in Sobibor in 1942.

These memories are more present when we listen to *Soul House*. All these traces of the paths surveyed, which awaken in us pictures of the houses where we slept in childhood, of the secret of our expectations.

To find and follow such traces, which are also lines of light and color, *Soul House* brings us closer, thread by thread, to the tradition of the Lyon Master Craftsmen, manufacturers of fabrics of gold, of silver and silk, their companions in work and in misery, their families and young girls, who worked day and night on the historic slopes of the Croix-Rousse, long before the French Revolution. Those that from 1786 collectively wrote their despair and their requests in Notebooks of Grievances, respectfully addressed to the King and to the National Assembly... they were already the predecessors of the Canuts, the insurgents of 1831.

laughing silver thread on a silk core; shades of petals freshly fallen from yellow roses; green silk (...) tone on tone these blue moiré threads; piece of water piece of silk

thread of water; thread of rain; thread of sisterly silk

Here Gansel gives us a whole history of the art of weaving, of the powers of their scriptures, which celebrate the beauty, the subtlety, and the precious abundance of materials and colors. A history of workers' knowledge, echoes of their words, their sufferings and their aspirations: recalling their labors, their struggles and their exiles.

Drawing on the sources of *Soul House*, I too found again the way to Paradou, to the house of Ladislas Mandel where Gansel had taken me. The simple and generous welcome of the great scholar, linguist, and typographer was an invaluable gift and teaching to me. He suggested that I choose one of the stones from his garden to carve. Both of us heard his praise of calligraphy, of the trace of the brush or the stroke of the pen, barely a breath, a time of inner and deep breathing.

This breath, this slight line bordered by light: the outline of the "thin black wings" of migratory birds, at the dawn of the summer solstice. Writing of the great migrations—the birds have gone very far to Antarctica, and on the cliffs of the island the native burrows are empty.

on the damp peat there is the scent of tall mint recently pulled up for when the Arctic terns will come back to make their nests –

Michèle Ganem Gumpel
March–April, 2023

Notes to the poems

leave no trace
The quotations "where one takes shelter. Finds refuge." and "to live leaving no trace" are from Walter Benjamin's *Pariser Passagen*. The quotation "reorganizing space and through it time" is from Paolo F. de Moraes Farias: *Arabic Medieval Inscriptions from the Republic of Mali* (Oxford University Press, 2003).

muʿallaqāt: the hanging odes
An early English translation of these lines from Imru' al-Qays's poem done by Lady Anne Blunt and Wilfrid Scawen Blunt, in their book *The Seven Golden Odes of Pagan Arabia*, printed by the Chiswick Press (London, 1903), reads as follows:

> How many singers before me! Are there yet songs unsung?
> Dost thou, my sad soul, remember, where was her dwellingplace?
> ...
> Doubting I paused in the pastures, seeking her camel-tracks,
> ...
> There on the sand lay the hearth-stones, black in their emptiness,

a shelter to deposit a soul's word
The epigraph to this poem is from Lalla Romano, translated from the Italian by Philippe Giraudon, in *Jeune est le temps* (Éditions de la Différence, collection Orphée, 1994).

house of earth house of silk (III, litered with petals)
This poem references textiles exhibited at the Museum of Textiles, Lyon.

to inhabit beauty against all odds
Gansel had selected and translated quotations from Yehudi Menuhin's memoir for the book *Le Violon de la Paix*, illustrated by Myfanwy Pavelic and published in 2000 by Éditions Alternatives in the Pollen collection, created and curated by Suzanne Bukiet (1928–2016).

Acknowledgments

My deep gratitude to the editors of the following journals where earlier versions of these translations appeared for the first time:

Asymptote — "to make a word habitable"

The Common — "post-script"

New Poetry in Translation [World Poetry Review] — "to inhabit beauty," "a house over there," "nomadic house," and "leave no trace"

Thanks to Simon Richard Wilson and Lis McLoughlin for taking five of these poems—"a house to come back to against all odds," "an outcrop of peat and rocks," "puffins," "Farne Islands early August," and "like a message to N.D."—for the anthology *Migrations and Home: The Elements of Place* (NatureCulture, 2023).

Thanks also to Peter Constantine and Brian Sneeden and their students, also to Pauline Levy Valensi, for helping me become a better translator. Extra appreciation to Matvei Yankelevich, my editor, for his patience, encouragement, and expertise. I am grateful to Michèle Ganem Gumpel for introducing me to Mireille Gansel and her life-changing writing, also for 45 years of generosity, friendship, and love. Lastly, thanks Stu for always being there for me and helping me find *le mot juste*.

— JSS

Mireille Gansel has won major awards for both her translations of German and Vietnamese poets, and for some of her seven books of poetry. Her lyrical memoir, *Translation as Transhumance*—published in an English translation by Ros Schwartz—has contributed significantly to the field of translation studies. She received the Veu Lliure 2021 Prize from the Catalan PEN. In 2018, Mireille became the Laureate of the Great Prize of Translation Etienne Dolet-Sorbonne Université. Other awards include the Khoury-Ghata poetry prize, the Gérald de Nerval translation prize, an English PEN Award, and a French Voices Award.

Joan Seliger Sidney's books of poetry include *Body of Diminishing Motion*, *Bereft and Blessed*, and *The Way the Past Comes Back*. Her translations, poems, and essays have appeared or are forthcoming in many literary journals and anthologies, including *The Common* and *Asymptote*, and have been nominated for Pushcart Prizes. She is Writer-in-Residence at University of Connecticut's Center for Judaic Studies and has received several fellowships from the Connecticut Commission on the Arts, the Vermont Studio Center, and a Visiting Faculty Fellowship from Yale University.

Fanny Howe is the author of many books of poetry and prose. She has received fellowships and awards from the National Endowment for the Arts, the National Poetry Foundation, the California Council for the Arts, the Guggenheim Foundation and was awarded the Ruth Lilly Poetry Prize in 2009. Howe taught for the University of California at San Diego, where she is professor emerita.

Born at the time of the Second World War to a French-Jewish family, **Michèle Ganem Gumpel**, a retired professor at the University of Grenoble Alpes, has devoted her teachings and publications to contemporary expressions of memory and questions of time.

This book was typeset in Domaine, a contemporary blend of traditional French and British typographic genres, designed by Kris Sowersby for Klim. The artwork on the cover is a work by Lebadang (1921–2015), used courtesy of Myshu Labadang's Collection. Cover design by Andrew Bourne; typesetting by Don't Look Now. Printed and bound by BALTO Print in Lithuania.

WORLD POETRY

Jean-Paul Auxeméry
Selected Poems
tr. Nathaniel Tarn

Maria Borio
Transparencies
tr. Danielle Pieratti

Jeannette L. Clariond
Goddesses of Water
tr. Samantha Schnee

Jacques Darras
John Scotus Eriugena at Laon
tr. Richard Sieburth

Olivia Elias
Chaos, Crossing
tr. Kareem James Abu-Zeid

Jerzy Ficowski
Everything I Don't Know
tr. Jennifer Grotz & Piotr Sommer
PEN AWARD FOR POETRY IN TRANSLATION

Antonio Gamoneda
Book of the Cold
tr. Katherine M. Hedeen &
Víctor Rodríguez Núñez

Mireille Gansel
Soul House
tr. Joan Seliger Sidney

Óscar García Sierra
Houston, I'm the problem
tr. Carmen Yus Quintero

Phoebe Giannisi
Homerica
tr. Brian Sneeden

Zuzanna Ginczanka
On Centaurs and Other Poems
tr. Alex Braslavsky

Leeladhar Jagoori
What of the Earth Was Saved
tr. Matt Reeck

*Nakedness Is My End:
Poems from the Greek Anthology*
tr. Edmund Keeley

Jazra Khaleed
The Light That Burns Us
ed. Karen Van Dyck

Judith Kiros
O
tr. Kira Josefsson

Dimitra Kotoula
The Slow Horizon That Breathes
tr. Maria Nazos

Maria Laina
Hers
tr. Karen Van Dyck

Maria Laina
Rose Fear
tr. Sarah McCann

Perrin Langda
A Few Microseconds on Earth
tr. Pauline Levy Valensi

Afrizal Malna
Document Shredding Museum
tr. Daniel Owen

Manuel Maples Arce
Stridentist Poems
tr. KM Cascia

Ennio Moltedo
Night
tr. Marguerite Feitlowitz

Meret Oppenheim
*The Loveliest Vowel Empties:
Collected Poems*
tr. Kathleen Heil

Giovanni Pascoli
Last Dream
tr. Geoffrey Brock
RAIZISS/DE PALCHI TRANSLATION AWARD

Gabriel Pomerand
Saint Ghetto of the Loans
tr. Michael Kasper &
Bhamati Viswanathan

Rainer Maria Rilke
Where the Paths Do Not Go
tr. Burton Pike

Elisabeth Rynell
Night Talks
tr. Rika Lesser

George Sarantaris
Abyss and Song: Selected Poems
tr. Pria Louka

Seo Jung Hak
The Cheapest France in Town
tr. Megan Sungyoon

Ardengo Soffici
Simultaneities & Lyric Chemisms
tr. Olivia E. Sears

Paul Verlaine
Before Wisdom: The Early Poems
tr. Keith Waldrop & K. A. Hays

Uljana Wolf
kochanie, today i bought bread
tr. Greg Nissan

Ye Lijun
My Mountain Country
tr. Fiona Sze-Lorrain

Verónica Zondek
Cold Fire
tr. Katherine Silver